POCKET
NEGOTIATOR

The
Economist
Books

POCKET
NEGOTIATOR

GAVIN KENNEDY

*The essentials of
successful negotiation
from A to Z*

THE ECONOMIST IN ASSOCIATION WITH
HAMISH HAMILTON LTD
Published by the Penguin Group
Penguin Books Ltd, 27 Wrights Lane, London W8 5TZ, England
Penguin Books USA Inc., 375 Hudson Street, New York,
New York 10014, USA
Penguin Books Australia Ltd, Ringwood, Victoria, Australia
Penguin Books Canada Ltd, 10 Alcorn Avenue, Toronto,
Ontario, Canada M4V 3B2
Penguin Books (NZ) Ltd, 182–190 Wairau Road, Auckland 10,
New Zealand

Penguin Books Ltd, Registered Offices:
Harmondsworth, Middlesex, England

First published by The Economist Books Ltd 1993
Reprinted by Hamish Hamilton Ltd in association with
The Economist Books Ltd 1994

3 5 7 9 10 8 6 4 2

Printed and bound in Great Britain by
William Clowes Limited, Beccles and London

A CIP catalogue record for this book is available
from the British Library

ISBN 0-241-00238-9

CONTENTS

PREFACE

Pocket Negotiator helps you to understand and manage the process of negotiation. It is meant to be consulted more than once, dipped into and thought about before, or even during, your negotiations.

It is an *aide-mémoire*, not a treatise. It suggests insights rather than elaborate concepts. It is full of practical tips. It also explains some academic theories without becoming detached from the real world of business negotiation. *Pocket Negotiator* is a not a guide for bluffing your way through a negotiation. There is little that is meant to be "Machiavellian" in its approach. Bluffs are usually counter-productive and best left to unserious amateurs and armchair voyeurs of the real world of business.

In so far as manipulative ploys are identified the aim is to prepare you for what might come across the table rather than arm you with tricks to trap the other negotiator. A ploy identified is a ploy neutralised. *Pocket Negotiator* is a practical as well as an informative guide to negotiating.

Many people have influenced my work on negotiation in the past 22 years – too many to mention on this occasion – and I hope they will forgive me this once for not fully acknowledging my many debts to them. I have space to make only one exception to this exclusion, namely my colleague and friend, Colin Rose, in Victoria, Australia. In two areas in particular Colin has contributed much to my thinking and practice. First on the different styles of negotiation, and second on seeing the "Four Phases" of negotiation from the perspective of parties seeking what they want. The former is summarised in the opening essay on handling difficult negotiators (although Colin may enter a disclaimer in respect of my interpretation and presentation).

Gavin Kennedy

INTRODUCTION

We often find ourselves in conflict with others, such as customers who want it yesterday, rivals who can supply it today, suppliers who will not deliver to our deadlines and certainly not when they promised, customers who claim that they never received what we despatched a week ago, colleagues who cannot see us when we need them and cannot see what we know is in their best interests, employees who want more pay (and time off), families who spend it before we earn it, children who think we are a bottomless pit, and bosses who think they know whose fault it is.

We negotiate to find acceptable solutions to these and other problems. We start with two solutions (yours and mine) to the same problem, be it two prices, two shares, two delivery dates, two wage rates, two specifications, two times to meet, two budget levels, two amounts of pocket money, and so on. When we negotiate we search for one solution with which we can both agree. It is unlikely to be the same as either of the solutions each of us started with; if it were then somebody would have given in, which is not a negotiation.

We all have considerable negotiation experience. We become adults after a long apprenticeship in negotiation: from the quantity of cabbage we must eat before we get some ice cream (our first negotiations are in the kitchen not the board room), through to the reward for a tidy room, who we can play with and where, or what we can watch on television. As teenagers we negotiate as part of our courtship ritual, including "your place or mine?" By the time we enter employment we are ready for the constant negotiation over the allocation of resources.

Mostly we do not think about negotiation, any more than we think about its alternatives, such as persuasion, giving in, instruction, haggling, coercion and joint problem-solving. We switch into and out of negotiation without thinking, sometimes getting what we want and sometimes not. Yet, if we tap the rich seam of our own experience, apply ourselves to some obvious but often forgotten techniques, and begin to think about what we normally do without thought, we can improve our negotiating performance dramatically.

That is the main purpose of reading *Pocket Negotiator*: to improve your performance as a negotiator. To help you achieve this result a number of short essays are included along with the A–Z section. The selection of topics for the essays is based on the author's experience of the most common questions asked at seminars. They are by no means comprehensive, nor are they meant to be, but if negotiators continually ask these questions, there is a benefit in including them in a book designed to be kept close to, if not inside, your pocket.

The Pocket Management series is designed to take the mystique out of business jargon in a stimulating and entertaining way. Other titles in the series include:

Pocket Finance
Pocket MBA
Pocket Manager
Pocket Marketing
Pocket Strategy

Part 1

ESSAYS

WHAT IS THE BASIS FOR THE DIFFERENT STYLES OF NEGOTIATION?

Negotiation is about trading. This distinguishes it from other forms of decision-making. In negotiation there is an explicit trade: I get some of what I want and you get some of what you want. We trade what we have that others want for what we want from them.

We do not, however, negotiate in a contextual vacuum. Because we happen to be meeting to make a decision, it does not follow necessarily that either of us attempts to make explicit trades. We can seek to resolve the matter by various means, including trying to force the other to capitulate. Nor need we abide by any notion of "fairness". Indeed, I can attempt to exploit you by silver-tongued sales techniques, or by playing on your ignorance, or by threatening you with dire consequences if you resist my demands.

Where does this leave the person who wants to trade to arrive at a solution when up against somebody else who does not? This gives us the style dimension, divided between those who want something for nothing (Red stylists) and those who trade something for something (Blue stylists). Think of this dimension as a continuum, with extreme Red stylists at one end and extreme Blue stylists at the other. In between the extremes there are varying shades of redness, purple and blueness.

Red stylists are characterised by their beliefs about how decisions can be made to work for them. They:

- see all negotiations as "one-off" contests;
- seek to win by domination;
- believe that more for them inevitably means less for you (but that is your problem not theirs);
- are prone to bluffs, ploys, "dirty tricks", even coercion;
- want something for nothing.

Whereas Blue stylists:

- see any negotiation in its long-term context;
- seek to succeed by co-operation;
- believe more for you means more for them (which is a joint gain for both of you);
- eschew manipulative techniques, preferring instead to address each party's interests using negotiable tradables;
- will only trade something for something.

In practice, the clash between Red and Blue styles leads to varying outcomes. Sometimes the Blue stylist is intimidated into submission by an overtly aggressive display by the Red stylist; sometimes the Red stylist achieves the same result (something for nothing) by stealth and by hiding his or her Red intentions.

This creates the following matrix.

Red	Blue
Aggressive	Submissive
Takes something for nothing	Gives something for nothing
Covert	Assertive
Finesses something for nothing	Trades something for something

You can think of individuals who predominantly display one of the characteristics shown in the matrix. Alternatively, and more revealingly perhaps, you should think of occasions when you have displayed all four variants.

- Any time that you make an unconditional offer you are a submissive Blue.
- Whenever you make a unilateral demand, with no offer of anything in return, you are an aggressive Red.
- On those occasions when you exploit somebody because you cannot resist the temptation, you are a covert Red.
- When you negotiate using conditional proposals only (if you . . . then . . .) you are an assertive Blue.

HOW SHOULD WE HANDLE DIFFICULT NEGOTIATORS?

Everybody we negotiate with is difficult to some degree; they do not agree with us for a start and insist on being less than enthusiastic about what we want. In this context difficult negotiators are taken to mean people who behave in an extremely difficult fashion, who are usually aggressive Red stylists, with manners (or lack of them) to match. You know them when you deal with them and the question is how you should handle them in a decision-making context.

That, of course, is the problem. You have come to negotiate and they have not. Their version of a solution requires you to give in, give them what they want (all of it) and go home quietly.

Many inexperienced decision-makers behave aggressively because they confuse aggression with toughness. They adopt aggressive behaviour to get what they want and because some people submit to them, they find that aggression works and so they adopt it whenever they want something.

You have to break the connection between winning and intimidation. If you do not do this, you join the submissive Blues who reinforce aggressiveness by rewarding it.

First, you will have to grab their attention so that you can assert unambiguously that there are only two ways they are going to get what they want – through the merits of their case or through trading – and that you will not submit to intimidation, bullying, or threats. Second, you have the choice when dealing with difficult negotiators of matching or contrasting their style.

Style matching is risky because it responds in kind to difficult negotiators' behaviour and "who started it" can easily get lost in the fog of insults and threats. It can work, however, if carefully controlled. For example, a bitter strike may have to be fought out to the finish (or look as if it is going to be) to bring the strikers to their senses and back to the negotiating table. Of course this could go horribly wrong, particularly if the strike (or terrorism, and so on) becomes the supreme issue instead of the merits of the case or the principle of trading.

The purpose of style matching is to avoid constructive submission and to leave open the alternative route to a settlement.

Style contrast is also risky because the contrast in styles could be read by difficult negotiators as constructive submission, in other words they perceive that you are submitting in all but name. Instead of responding in kind to their outrageous behaviour you should:

- speak more quietly than they do;
- speak more slowly than they do;
- give way to their interruptions, but pause for a few seconds each time they finish;
- not respond in kind if they swear;
- not argue with their attacks on you and their apportioning of blame;
- not defend yourself against ascribed motives;
- ignore all threats;
- respond positively but specifically and without rancour to any blue moves they make, even in the midst of their Red-dominated activities;
- not respond at all to their Red moves, other than to say "no";
- affirm whenever appropriate the two principles on which you will agree to a solution (merits of the case and trading).

Your assertive Blue message will eventually get through (see SKINNER'S PIGEON).

- Toughness is not a synonym for shouting abuse, threatening and intimidation.
- Toughness is based on an absolute and patient firmness of purpose.

How do we deal with covert Red negotiators?

The answer is: not without difficulty. The problem is that most covert Red negotiators do not start off with the intention of cheating you (some do, of course). The majority find it impossible to resist the temptation to do so. The opportunity to cheat creeps up on them without warning and faced with a safe "steal" they cannot resist the temptation.

The covert Red and the assertive Blue are easily confused. The fact is that you do not know whether negotiators are going to exploit you if they are unaware themselves of how they will react if the opportunity to exploit you arises. This puts you at a disadvantage, but it is one you cannot avoid. You do not know for sure how you would react if a similar opportunity arises with the people you are dealing with; everyone has the potential to be tempted into being covert Red in certain circumstances.

Hence you could be dealing with apparently assertive Blue negotiators, characterised by:

- a cool but firm tone;
- respectful negotiating manners;
- patience in respect of the pace of your negotiation;
- an analytical rather than emotional approach;
- demonstrable listening skills.

In short, they are behaving just like you are.

These negotiators may intend to exploit you but their behaviour gives you no clues because their intentions are deliberately hidden from you (that is why they are covert). They may have no intention of cheating but cannot help it when the opportunity arises, perhaps on this single occasion. Their behaviour up to that moment is genuine but they switch to the covert Red role without revealing what they have done.

If you think that you are dealing with other

assertive Blues, you expose yourself to exploitation by revealing your expectations – even your interests – believing that it is safe to do so with these people (who are clearly not aggressive Red stylists). You carelessly offer movement on the implicit understanding that they will reciprocate; after all, you assume, they know it is a negotiation which is settled on the basis of trading not conceding. You reveal the following and that is when they strike.

- You desperately require their services. They increase their entry price and charge for add-ons when you accept it.
- Your budget is in surplus with no carry-over provisions to the next quarter. They quote a premium price despite your early payment.
- You are in trouble with your cash flow. They insist on advance payment.

Most covert Red proposals are willingly accepted by their victims; it is so easy to switch to the role of submissive Blue. So how do you handle them? Basically by never slipping out of the assertive Blue role which insists that everything is traded not conceded.

First, you must use Blue signals to test for covert Red intentions. A signal addresses the major strategic question of all negotiators: how to indicate a willingness to move without giving in. Signals, by a shift in emphasis from the affirmative defence of an opening position to a tentative willingness to consider moving, indicate that movement is possible providing it is not interpreted as you giving in.

- From demanding full compensation you signal that you require some compensation.
- From rejecting a demand as impossible you signal that it would be contrary to normal policy.
- From rejecting a general application of a principle you signal a willingness to discuss specific instances where it might be applicable.

The key is in how the other negotiators respond to your signal: if they rubbish it, you have a revealed Red stylist; if they respond positively they might be covert Red. And that is how it must remain; no matter what they appear to be, you never know if they are genuinely assertive Blue or potentially covert Red.

But all is not beyond hope of resolution. It depends on what you do next. You must now consider how you make your proposals.

Every negotiator has a Red side. If somebody offers us what we want for nothing we would surely take it.

- Suppose we made a proposal that only consisted of a condition (which states what we want). What is the nature of this proposal? Surely an aggressive Red stylist's attempt to get something for nothing.
- Suppose we made a proposal that only consisted of an offer (which gives them what they want). What is the nature of this proposal? Surely a submissive Blue stylist's free gift concession giving away something for nothing.

Thus these two proposals by themselves are the currency of either the aggressive Red or the submissive Blue stylist. They are like the two elements sodium and chlorine, which are poisonous to humans if ingested separately but which are also the foundation of life (salt) when ingested together.

The assertive Blue negotiator is in an analogous situation. Separately, the condition and the offer are the antithesis of decision by negotiation, but together they constitute the very essence of what negotiation is about. Combine them into a conditional proposal and the assertive negotiator is totally protected whatever the style coming across the table, overt or covert.

Condition
Your Red side stating
what you want

Offer
Your Blue side stating
what they want

"If you give me what I want . . . then I will give you what you want."

You can think of the conditional proposal as a purple style (a bit of Red and a bit of Blue, the proportions depending on the terms you are attempting to strike for a deal).

Conditional proposals consisting of your Red conditions and your Blue offers are purple defences against any Red plays, whether openly aggressive or covertly snatched. Conditionality asserts that they cannot get what they want from you without you getting what you want from them.

The conditional proposal:

- stumps the aggressive Red stylist to the extent that you mean it;
- poses no threat to the submissive Blues because they are too used to giving things away for nothing. This way they get something back (you never meant to exploit them did you?);
- flummoxes the covert Reds because to challenge the trading principle they would have to reveal their Red intentions and by definition the covert cannot do that;
- is no problem at all for genuine assertive Blues because they apply the trading principle themselves in all of their dealings.

WHAT IS THE ROLE OF MANIPULATIVE PLOYS?

There is a considerable market in offering "street-wise" advice on negotiating. For a lot of people negotiation is about "dirty tricks", ploys, gambits and so-called "tactics" and they are prepared to pay good money to hear about it.

Unfortunately much of this advice is unhelpful. It is true that learning about the manipulative approach has something to commend it, not least because any exposure to regular negotiation in business will demonstrate all kinds of variations in tactical ploys being tried upon you. Because negotiation is an unscripted interaction with no "rules", no appeals and no comebacks, it could appear on the surface that the manipulative approach is the dominant one and something you must become adept in quickly if you are to do well.

These approaches, however, are unhelpful if you confuse identifying what some people might try to do to you in a negotiation with what you must learn to do to others. Courses that teach tactical manipulation suffer from at least three drawbacks.

- You forget the appropriate ploy for the situation.
- You apply the wrong ploy for the situation.
- The situation was not covered in the course.

In the A–Z entries numerous ploys are illustrated but there is a difference between being introduced to the manipulative ploys that may be used against you and encouraging you to become manipulative. A ploy identified by you in the course of a negotiating exchange is a ploy neutralised. Moreover, if you recognise that the negotiators are attempting to manipulate you it should alert you to their Red intentions.

All ploys, tricks and bluffs have a single aim: to influence the perception you have of their power because perceptions of power and your expectations are linked together.

- The less power relative to you that you perceive them to have, the greater your expectation of the outcome.
- The more power that you perceive them to have relative to you, the less your expectation of the outcome.

Manipulative negotiators have a strong incentive therefore to work on your perceptions of their power. It directly influences what you expect to result from the negotiation.

If you perceive your power to be:

- non-existent in the situation, you are likely to give up;
- negligible in the situation, you are likely to give in;
- balanced with theirs, you are likely to trade;
- overwhelming, you are likely to impose compliance.

All manipulative ploys can be divided into three main phases in a negotiation depending on their tactical roles.

- Dominance
- Shaping
- Closing

In phase one manipulators work to dominate you and the proceedings. They might:

- insist on preconditions;
- declare some issues non-negotiable;
- attempt to decide the AGENDA, its order and the timing unilaterally;
- behave in an aggressive Red style;
- hint at threats of SANCTIONS;
- disdainfully dismiss you, your products, your business, your views.

In phase two manipulators work to shape the deal in their favour. They might:

- play TOUGH GUY/NICE GUY;
- use SALAMI;
- use ADD-ON;
- try MOTHER HUBBARD;
- try RUSSIAN FRONT.

In phase three manipulators work to close the deal on their terms. They might:

- demand you SPLIT THE DIFFERENCE;
- claim it is "now or never";
- set a phoney DEADLINE;
- threaten with the "OR ELSE" close;
- bluff a WALK-OUT.

By identifying the likely ploys (and there are many more than the selection quoted above) you can win the battle to influence your perceptions.

If you know what the manipulators are about it makes it easier either to counter (every ploy has a counter) or to ignore (any ploy is weakened by being ignored).

If your perceptions are uninfluenced by the manipulators you can concentrate on negotiating the issues.

Part 2
A–Z

ADD-ON

A ploy to increase the quoted terms for a transaction. The add-on is a plausible extra, such as for delivery or fitting or for some necessary component (batteries, wires, plugs, and so on), added to the cost of the main item.

The technique is to quote basic prices only and then add on for ancillaries, or divide your product or service into component parts and set prices for the main components and add-on prices for the rest.

Counter: Find out what you get for your money before you give a BUYING SIGNAL.

ADJOURNMENT

The negotiator's equivalent of a time-out. You agree to terminate the current negotiating session and adjourn for a while: minutes in the corridor, hours in another room, days back at your own site, and so on. You need:

- a break to think about what has been said;
- to reconsider your position;
- to regroup your team;
- to consult with your advisers or more senior decision-makers;
- to put pressure on them if they are keen for a decision;
- to rest and recuperate.

Adjournments are risky because while absent, circumstances can change; for example, your rivals make irresistible proposals or they find a better product than yours.

Negotiators calling for an adjournment also create EXPECTATIONS that they may be unable to fulfil on their return. If you do no more than re-state your pre-adjournment position, you risk creating hostility.

Always make clear why you are adjourning. If they call for an adjournment, it is best to agree to one. Avoid "valedictory" exhortations and speeches once an adjournment is called. They waste TIME, and risk further ARGUMENT.

ADVANCE

Payment of part (a deposit) or all of the charge for services yet to be performed; but will the service be performed afterwards?

Avoid advance payments to people you do not know. If they are short of cash, they are unreliable. If, plausibly, they need money for materials, buy them yourself and deliver them to your premises not theirs.

If a reputable business wants an advance payment (get a signed and dated receipt), require a discount on the price at least equivalent to the interest you lose while they have your money. Banks do not lend money for nothing, so why should you?

AGENDA

An order of business. It sets out the sequence of the issues to be negotiated; it is a helpful organiser of what would otherwise be a wandering debate.

You can agree on the composition of an agenda but disagree on the order in which items will be discussed. One solution is to agree to negotiate the items in any order on the basis that "nothing is agreed until everything is agreed".

Extremely hostile relationships between negotiators preclude detailed agendas. But agreement to consider an agenda is a step forward, and the less specific the headings on the agenda, the more likely the parties are to agree to meet.

AGENT

Somebody who represents a PRINCIPAL to third parties. Used in real estate transactions and for the buying and selling of goods and services.

In some countries specific laws protect agents, making it difficult to terminate an agency – at least cheaply – if circumstances suggest you should do so. Many countries require foreigners to operate exclusively through nationals who act as commercial agents (see GO-BETWEEN), but some specifically prohibit the use of local agents (because of bribery scandals).

It is essential to know about local practices to avoid surprise penalties and unplanned jail sentences.

There are four important prerequisites in negotiating an agency contract.

1 Strictly define your agent's authority and the limits to your liability.
2 Strictly define the territory.
3 Reserve the right to terminate the agency:

- if sales and profit targets are not met;
- if payments are not made on time;
- if the agent is taken over by another party;
- if the agent is discovered to be in breach of trust;
- if the agent fails to maintain declared standards of quality.

4 Include a dated TERMINATION clause that enables you to re-assign the agency to another party, redefine the extent of the territory, renegotiate any of the terms of the agency, or take over direct distribution of your own product.

AGREEMENT
Preferred name for a contract. Agreements are on the angels' side of the TRUST boundary; contracts lie just over it. If agreed obligations are not met, call your agreement a contract.

Record what was agreed during the negotiation, not after you have dispersed. If you cannot agree what was agreed while you are together, it is unlikely that you will do so later. If you cannot agree, carry on negotiating until you can.

Record the agreement in any mutually acceptable form. All agreements should outline the action to be taken by each party to implement the agreement.

ALTERNATIVE
If the negotiated possibilities are inferior to the available alternatives, it is better to abandon an attempt to negotiate the differences (see BATNA).

The more alternatives you have the stronger your negotiating position.

AMBIGUITY

May be intentional or unintentional. Intentional ambiguities arise when there is a need for a face-saving formula to break a DEADLOCK: "You interpret it your way and we will interpret it our way."

Employer–union PROCEDURE agreements state that: "The employers have the right to manage their enterprises and the unions have the right to exercise their functions." These rights overlap, and depending on the circumstances and the economic climate, one side's interpretation could trespass on the other's.

APPLES AND PEARS

Proposals may be substitutes but they need not be comparable.

With several proposals it is difficult to make accurate comparisons because the proposals may not be comparable at all. Each proposal varies in a different respect to the other. They are similar in that they are fruit, but one is an apple and the other is a pear.

ARBITRATION

Use of a private tribunal or person to adjudicate a dispute between parties instead of recourse to litigation.

Many countries have a legal basis for the use of arbitrators, sometimes making the decision of an arbitrator legally binding on the parties (for example, labour law in Australia and the USA). Sometimes it is a non-binding voluntary arrangement when it arises out of a conciliation process (such as ACAS, the UK's Advisory, Conciliation and Arbitration Service).

If you are unable to resolve a dispute, refer the issue to a mutually acceptable third party who, for a fee, receives submissions from each side (written or oral), exercises judgment and then pronounces a verdict. Alternatively, you and the disputing party can nominate one person each,

and the two nominees then choose a third person
to form an arbitration panel.

Negotiators cease to influence the outcome if
their dispute goes to arbitration. Their case stands
or falls on its merits as judged by the arbitrator.
The arbitrator may choose some COMPROMISE
between the parties' final proposals. (See PENDU-
LUM ARBITRATION.)

The International Chamber of Commerce provides an arbitration service for commercial contracts (for details contact: ICC Court of
Arbitration, 38 Cours Albert 1er, 75008 Paris).

ARGUMENT

Argument is a destructive form of debate.

Some negotiations never get beyond argument.
We can only negotiate PROPOSALS. Destructive
argument consists of:

- emotive language;
- point scoring;
- blaming, swearing and cursing;
- attacking the other negotiator's integrity;
- questioning their authority;
- interrupting;
- shouting down;
- mocking;
- generally being obstructive.

Argument prevents proposals being formulated, or if formulated, prevents their being considered constructively.

ASPIRATIONS

The world is full of unfulfilled ambitions. Some
research shows that high aspirations produce better results than low aspirations; you never get
more than you ask for. Other research shows
high aspirations result in a higher incidence of
DEADLOCK.

Balance the prize of high aspirations with the
PRICE of unfulfilled ambition.

When a party with high aspirations meets a
party of low aspirations, the less ambitious party

sometimes gives way: ambition becomes self-fulfilling. Alternatively, the overambitious negotiator antagonises the less ambitious. Worms turn; they fight back; sometimes they gain enough courage from their anger to reverse their low aspirations.

You should not necessarily aim low; you usually get less than you aim for.

Balance the prize of a poor reward with the price of easily fulfilled ambition.

ASSUMPTIONS
In business, and in affairs of the heart, assumptions are inevitable.

- Check out your assumptions before acting upon them.
- Ask QUESTIONS.
- Listen to the answers for what they tell you about your assumptions.

ASSUMPTIVE CLOSE
A seller's close ploy. The seller asks a question which assumes that the prospective buyer has decided to purchase. If the buyer answers the question, he (or she) commits himself to buy.

- Will you collect or shall we deliver?
- Is it cash or charge?
- Do you want them in batches of 50, or 100?

If you are buying, seek additional movement from the seller before you give a BUYING SIGNAL. To block the assumptive close tell the seller: l am not in a position to answer these questions until I have decided whether to do business with you. First you must tell me what you propose in respect of the following.

AUCTION
System of selling that puts maximum pressure on buyers.

- In a regular auction buyers call out their bids in an ascending order. The last bidder wins.

- In a DUTCH AUCTION the first bidder wins. The auctioneer calls prices in a descending order (but see also common misuse of this term).
- In a "Vickery sealed-bid auction" the highest bidder wins at the second highest bidder's PRICE.

AUTHORITY

Negotiators without authority leave you vulnerable if the higher authority seeks additional concessions from you in exchange for an AGREEMENT. Avoid this by:

- asking the negotiators whether they have the full authority to settle. Do not necessarily believe the answer you get;
- holding back something in the proposal for that final traded CONCESSION to get agreement.

When asked if you have authority when you have not, say yes. Take an ADJOURNMENT to "consider the proposal" but use the opportunity to refer it to the decision-makers. Claim on your return to the meeting that the required changes resulted from your own consideration of the total package.

To assess authority levels, ask the following questions.

❏ What are your procedures for making decisions of this nature?

❏ Who in your company participates in these decisions?

❏ How long do decisions of this nature normally take?

AVOIDANCE-AVOIDANCE MODEL

Application of an insight from psychology to negotiation.

Briefly, people faced with two relatively unattractive choices try to avoid both. The closer they are to an unattractive choice, the more they try to avoid making it.

For example, a company's choices are to:

- settle on the union's terms;
- stick to its current position and thus risk the costs of a STRIKE.

A company wishing to avoid both choices seeks a COMPROMISE: a wage rise smaller than the union's demands, but bigger than its own opening OFFER.

The union's debate STRATEGY aims to:

- increase the company's tendency to avoid a strike;
- reduce the company's tendency to avoid meeting the union's current demand.

The union asserts that the costs of a strike are higher than the company's own estimates (SECONDARY BOYCOTTS), or that the company's competitors are raising their wage costs, thus reducing the RISK of a competitive disadvantage if it meets additional costs of the union's claim.

The company's debate strategy aims to:

- increase the union's tendency to avoid a deadlock;
- decrease the union's tendency to avoid accepting the company's last offer.

BAGATELLE

A presentational ploy to overcome resistance to major changes perceived to be too expensive, onerous or unacceptable to the other party.

The bagatelle is used by sellers of anything relatively expensive. To protect yourself from the bagatelle, always GROSS up to the full cost (PRICE per slice times the number of slices). To use the bagatelle, break down the total cost of your product into small slices.

For instance, sell paper by the sheet; hospital insurance by the daily charge; cable TV by the cost per hour; telephone calls in three minute units (call Timbuktoo for only $3.52).

Timeshare companies use a brilliant bagatelle: "A week in Acapulco for ever, for the cost of a week in Acapulco."

BALLOON

When the entire loan, plus the accumulated interest, is paid off in one "balloon" payment on a specified date, instead of in regular instalments.

Lend on balloon terms if you want a large lump sum (the loan plus interest) at some date in the future. You are vulnerable if the borrower does not make provision to repay by the due date and their assets do not cover the loan plus accumulated interest.

Borrow on balloon terms if you expect a large sum (for example, inheritance, sale of an asset) by the due date. If you fail to make provision for repayment you put at RISK your assets.

Lend on balloon terms by:

- requiring the borrower to pledge an asset against the loan and the accumulated interest;
- insisting on a standard security over the asset;
- only lending what you can wait a long time for;
- regularly inspecting the pledged asset.

BANK

Banks lend money that does not belong to them. If they do not lend, they go bust. If they lend any amount of money at a loss to somebody who cannot pay back what they borrow they also go bust.

Negotiating a loan to finance your lifestyle can be disastrous. You will end up broke, as interest payments gobble up your income (if you have any).

BARGAINING

Getting something you value highly for something you value less. Bargaining is based on exchanging something for something.

When you buy food in exchange for cash you value the food more than you do the cash, otherwise you would stay hungry. The seller values the cash more than the food, otherwise they would do without the cash. At the moment of the TRADE you each get a bargain.

To bargain, discover what you have that the other party values highly and what they have that you want.

BARGAINING CONTINUUM

Illustrates the relationship between the offers of two negotiators. The first OFFER we make is not the final offer that we might make.

We open with our entry point; where we are prepared to move to is our exit point. The distance between them is our negotiable range.

Figure 1 **Bargaining continuum**

| ENTRY | EXIT | NO DEAL | EXIT | ENTRY |

| ENTRY | | EXIT | | |

| | EXIT | | | ENTRY |

- The distance between our entry point and theirs is the bargaining continuum.
- If our exit points overlap we could settle anywhere in the overlap. This is the settlement area.
- If our exit points do not meet or overlap we are unlikely to settle.

BARGAINING LANGUAGE

Some forms of language help negotiators, others do not. The following language does not help.

Q: I'll increase my OFFER by ten. How about that?
A: Okay, we'll throw in two extra terminals.
Q: If I improve the payback period, will that do?
A: We'll cover the insurance costs, okay?

These are unconditional offers. They do not require anything in exchange.

An unconditional offer is a movement towards giving in. If they are moving at "no cost to you", keep them moving by asking for more.

Use CONDITIONAL LANGUAGE.

- If you pay in 21 days, then I'll increase the offer to ten.
- If you buy the standard software, then I'll include an extra terminal.
- If you sign the order now, then I'll improve the payback period.
- If you pay for full security cover, than I'll abate the insurance charge.

BARTER

Exchange of goods and services without using cash. Sometimes prevalent in times of war, revolution, hyperinflation and other disasters. Anybody with anything to TRADE can try bartering to get what they want. Children barter toys because they have no cash. In the "soft" or "black" economy people trade their labour for food, their surplus food for timber, their surplus household fixtures for whatever they can get for them.

Barter is less efficient than cash, if cash is available, and requires haggling skills.

Remember: It is not what it is worth to you that counts, but what it is worth to the person that wants it.

BATNA
See below.

BEST ALTERNATIVE TO A NEGOTIATED AGREEMENT
Commonly referred to by its acronym BATNA.

How does the proposal match your realistic alternatives? The more attractive your alternatives to the proposed AGREEMENT the more POWER you have. The fewer your alternatives, and the less attractive they are compared with the results of negotiation, the less power you have.

The following will help to develop your BATNA.

- ❏ List anything you could conceivably do if you fail to reach an acceptable agreement.
- ❏ Convert the most promising alternatives into practical options.
- ❏ Select your single best option. This is your BATNA.
- ❏ Judge all proposals against this BATNA.
- ❏ If the OFFER is better than your BATNA, consider accepting the offer.
- ❏ If the offer is worse than your BATNA, negotiate for improvement.
- ❏ If they will not improve their offer, exercise your BATNA.

BID
Puts maximum pressure on a supplier.

Suppliers bid on a ONE-OFFER-ONLY basis, quoting their "best PRICE" for the specified work. Bids are expected to contain a minimum of PADDING, provided buyers enforce a one-offer-only procedure and there is no collusion among the bidders.

Allowing bidders to negotiate their bids induces them to pad their first bid, until they see what the competition is quoting.

If further discussion is allowed this weakens the price squeeze effects on the seller.

BID/NO BID

Bidding costs can be high. These costs are recouped if the bid is successful.

If you do not bid, you do not win business. If you bid unsuccessfully you add to costs. Balancing winning bids with losing bids may not be enough. You must increase the bid win rate.

If, however, you are overloaded with work the last thing you need is more work. Bid high, and hope they say "no thanks".

Winning unprofitable bids is not good for business. Hence:

☐ What happens if you do not bid?
☐ What happens if you bid but lose?
☐ What happens if you bid and win?
☐ Is there any VULNERABILITY in the contract terms?
☐ Who are the competitors for the contract?
☐ What can you offer that is as good, different or better than the competition?
☐ Where are you vulnerable to competitive pressure?
☐ How can you influence the client to prefer your bid?
☐ Can you emphasise the relationship between in-service costs and initial PRICE?
☐ Can you repackage finance and credit?
☐ Can you highlight cost ADD-ONS of spurious specifications ("gold plating")?
☐ Can you offer better after-sales service?
☐ Can you demonstrate high-profile quality-assurance systems?

If the answers are positive, deploy resources for the bid. If they are marginal, compare with immediate alternative bids. If they are negative, or insufficiently positive, do not bid.

BID LAST

A ploy to maximise your minimal chances of doing better in a competitive bid situation.

If asked to bid competitively for business, and you eagerly send in your bid early, the buyer can use your bid to encourage others to improve upon it. Hence, bid last. Hand it over by reliable messenger at the very last moment that you can.

If the bidding develops into an AUCTION proceed as follows.

- Tell them to contact you last and ask for details of the lowest bid.
- Blow the best bid out of the water, or withdraw.
- Never bid more than once in a bid auction: bid last or not at all.

BLACKMAIL

Influencing another's behaviour by threats to expose something, or to damage something or someone they value. The blackmailer's STRATEGY is to threaten harm unless you comply with their demands.

As a TARGET you can choose to comply with, or resist, the blackmailer's demands. As a blackmailer you can choose to reprieve or punish the target.

There are costs to you in complying:

- paying money;
- changing a policy;
- releasing the blackmailer's cronies;
- refraining from doing something you would otherwise prefer to do.

The blackmailer may punish you out of vindictiveness (or to destroy evidence or a witness), or reprieve you if you comply.

If you resist, the costs to you of the blackmailer implementing his or her THREAT and inflicting the threatened punishment could involve such things as killing a hostage, destroying property, making public something about you, causing havoc, and so on.

You can also benefit from each choice.

- By complying you avoid the blackmailer's threat of punishment (NET of the consequences to your wealth, your policy preferences, respect for law and order, and so on).
- By resisting you avoid the costs of complying, and may avoid punishment (if the blackmailer is bluffing or is stymied by your resistance).

The outcome depends on the balance of probabilities of the alternative events occurring. The blackmailer aims to convince you that threats will be carried out if you do not comply. If you greatly value the threatened object (the victim, the business, the state of peace, your reputation), and believe that the threat is credible, you are persuaded to comply and not resist.

The blackmailer's tactics include enhancing the credibility of the threat (visibly preparing for war, for strikes and demonstrating a capacity for punitive actions). Credibility is also enhanced if there is an inevitability about the threat being imposed. For example, a third party inflicts the punishment automatically if the deadline is not met; or there is a record of imposing punishment in similar circumstances.

Tactics available to you are limited if the blackmailer's threat is unexpected (a kidnapping, a hijack), and you have little experience of dealing with the problem. Your tactics include the following.

- Reducing the value to the blackmailer of choosing to inflict punishment by encouraging belief in a positive pay-off for a reprieve.
- Convincing the blackmailer that you are ready to comply to delay punishment.
- Stalling while defences are marshalled against the costs of punishment (prepare for war, stockpile for a STRIKE, arrange alternative supplies, set the police to hunt the kidnapper, make public disclosures of the incidents the blackmailer is threatening to disclose, and so on).

Under the stress of maintaining vigilance for "tricks", or merely from reviewing the uncertain pay-offs of the exercise, blackmailers sometimes reduce their demands to encourage compliance. Experience shows that this encourages resistance, because it increases the net benefits to you of non-compliance.

Your willingness to resist depends on the relative pay-offs for compliance (C) and resistance (R). The relative balance between the pay-offs (net benefits) decides the appropriate action.

- If R > C you should resist.
- If C > R you should comply.
- If the RISK of punishment is minimal you should aim for a reprieve.

The blackmailer has a better chance of succeeding if the cost of compliance to you is not unreasonable and the compliance demand is realistic. Unrealistic compliance demands raise the net benefit of resistance.

BLAME CYCLE

Negotiators get bogged down in blame cycles, because identifying the guilty is easier than addressing the problem. Each side raises issues of less and less relevance to the immediate problem. The result is a destructive ARGUMENT.

Blame cycles are easy to slide into, are time-wasting, difficult to stop and destructive of a relationship. There are three things to tell anybody with a complaint.

- I am going to apologise on behalf of my people for the stress we have caused you.
- I am going to listen to what you have to say.
- With your help, I am going to put it right.

The complainer usually cools down, and becomes conciliatory.

BLOCKING OFFER

A disreputable ploy. A negotiator appears on the

scene offering much better terms than the one on offer. You stop a negotiation with the first buyer and switch to the new one. Once the old negotiation is dead, the new negotiator becomes difficult. There are "problems", unforeseen "difficulties", and newly significant "small print" in the proposal. You can either settle on the now much-reduced "better" terms or drop out of the negotiation.

If you try to settle and find the new negotiator drops out you will know it was only a blocking offer. He or she never intended to do a deal on any terms.

Counter: As a condition for dropping the first negotiation require the new negotiator to purchase an OPTION for a sum at least equivalent to the margin between his bid and the one you have from the first negotiator.

- ☐ If he settles on the agreed terms his money is set against the PRICE, if he does not, you keep his money.
- ☐ Prevarication suggests he is making a blocking offer.
- ☐ Go over his offer very carefully and watch out for LIFEBOAT CLAUSES.
- ☐ If there is anything in the offer giving him discretion, insist on its removal or amendment.

BLUFF
Much loved by scriptwriters with a passing acquaintance with the works of Machiavelli. It is almost always counter-productive. Bluffing is exhilarating from the security of your armchair, but it is cold sweat in the real world.

Avoiding bluffing does not mean you disclose your vulnerabilities. A called bluff is a credibility killer. Your prospects are dead from then on.

BOBBIN' AND WEAVIN'
A ploy to dodge a powerful assault on your weak flanks.

All positions have weaknesses. Other negotiators search for them. Damage avoidance is called for.

❑ **Parry the attack:** I could take up that point right now, but I prefer to do so when we have all the facts on the table.

❑ **Acknowledge the problems, but deny their importance:** Yes, you are right, we did miss that delivery, but against the entirety of our dealings, a missed delivery is hardly the decisive criterion of our competence.

❑ **Refer to TIME constraints:** I wish we had time to go into all the details and the special circumstances of that case, but if we did we would be here for hours.

❑ **Refer to NEED TO KNOW status:** To answer that point properly, I would need to disclose to you highly confidential details, so please do not pursue those matters further without the highest clearance from the boss.

BOULWARISM

A version of ONE-OFFER-ONLY applied to labour contracts. Named after Lemuel Boulware, vice-president of General Electric (USA), who introduced a negotiating stance that left no room for traditional methods of negotiation.

Boulwarism requires:

- a survey of employee opinion, ASPIRATIONS and attitudes;
- consideration of what the company wants to do in terms of wages and other conditions of employment;
- presentation of a total package to the employees which is non-negotiable.

Boulwarism is a major bogey in union mythology. Because it denies a formal BARGAINING role to the union, it produces considerable hostility, especially when introduced suddenly.

Boulwarism is likely to succeed where:

- the union leadership is discredited;
- the employees are recovering from a prolonged STRIKE;
- the market has visibly turned against the products;

- survival as a company is at the forefront of a majority of the employees' concerns;
- management intelligence has correctly estimated where the shop floor is willing to settle.

Boulwarism is not recommended for the faint of heart or managements that have not done their homework.

BRIBERY

Bribery is a crime. It is immoral. It is unethical. It is unfair. It is practised.

Bribery is corruption. It taints all who touch it. But in many parts of the world it is the way they do business. To cynics the boundary between bribery and paying for a service, or permission to do something, is blurred. You know you have crossed the boundary when you are caught.

Do not assume that everybody is on the take: any country's prisons are worse than its hotels.

Greedy people get sticky fingers. A GO-BETWEEN will bribe out of what he or she gets from you. Occasionally, a very important greedy person gets between you and your deal. It costs you a small fortune to get past him. Either pay up and shut up, or shop him and run.

BRINKMANSHIP

A high-RISK enforcement ploy. Foster Dulles, US secretary of state during the 1950s, exemplified diplomacy by brinkmanship. Here is a taste of his philosophy:

> You have to take chances for peace. Just as you must take chances in war. Some say we were brought to the verge of war. Of course we were brought to the verge of war. The ability to get to the verge without getting into war is the necessary art.

BROOKLYN OPTICIAN

A version of the ADD-ON ploy. The seller adds on costs until the buyer flinches. Supposedly worked to effect by a legendary optician in Brooklyn,

New York.

The lenses are $90 . . . each . . . the frame is $40 . . . for the basic shape, like your grandmother wore and $89 for a designer pair . . . plus $30 for fitting . . . in the shop, and $50 for a home visit . . . within four blocks, otherwise it's $5 a block extra . . . You can have them in five days for $10 . . . a day.

Regular brushed steel is $20 . . . a part and it's $45 if you want gold . . . leaf . . . 18 carat gold is $30 . . . a lens frame . . . plus state taxes . . .

Each pause gives the buyer an opportunity to call a halt, which if not taken, tells the seller to keep piling on the add-ons.

You can apply the ploy if you know your variables.

- My normal charge is $350 . . . weekends extra.
- That will be $90 . . . plus $30 for delivery . . . tomorrow . . . $45 today.
- The documentation charge is $120 . . . per head.

Counter: Flinch and cut in at the first pause.

BUYING SIGNAL

See one, stop your OFFER. Send one, and the offers stop.

Why? Because buying signals show a willingness to settle on the terms of the current offer, so why offer more?

Examples of buying signals include the following.

- Assumptive ownership: I'll make this room my study.
- Issuing instructions for delivery.
- Disappointment at lead times for possession.
- Concentrated attention to buying details.
- Asking QUESTIONS that relate the product or service directly to usage.
- Looking intently at the product. Get them to handle it, fly, sail, drive in it, touch, hear, smell it (the SIZZLE), and keep it in their sight

(every glance at it is another signal).
- Asking what their spouse/partner thinks.
- Showing good humour with their partner (the euphoria of the purchase).
- Positive responses to an ASSUMPTIVE CLOSE.

CAPITULATION
The ultimate CONCESSION.

CAR-BUYING PSYCHOLOGY
Professional car dealers have at least one advantage over you: they practise their technique several times a day, while you try it perhaps once every few years.

When buying a volume car, the seller tries to convince you that you can afford it; when buying a prestige car (Rolls-Royce, Mercedes, Jaguar) you try to persuade the seller that you can afford it. Either way, the seller has got you.

CASH
Instant, perfect liquidity. Also easy to lose through theft, accident and impulse. Insist on cash:

❒ Sooner rather than later.
❒ When dealing with unreliable, untrustworthy, or otherwise suspect people.
❒ When your banker has closed your account.
❒ When your creditors have charge of your assets.
❒ When you are unlikely to spend it.
❒ When the transaction is dodgy.
❒ When it is a no come-backs deal.

Refrain from accepting cash:

❒ When you are paid in dark alleys.
❒ When you can wait for your money.
❒ When you have a long journey to make.
❒ When you are an impulsive spender.

Pay cash:

❒ When you do not need a written record.
❒ When it helps reduce the PRICE.
❒ When you have too much cash on your person.
❒ When it gets you additional concessions.

Do not pay cash:

- ❏ When you need a written record.
- ❏ When you suspect the money is forged.
- ❏ When you might need to cancel the cheque before it is presented.
- ❏ When you are not sure who you are paying it to.
- ❏ When there is a delay between payment and the service.

CASH BEFORE PERFORMANCE

Used to ensure payments (see HOOKER'S PRIN-CIPLE). Use cash before performance (CBP):

- ❏ When you do not believe in credit.
- ❏ When your audiences might demand their money back.
- ❏ When the producer might scoot off with the takings.
- ❏ When you are into high living.
- ❏ When you are only hours ahead of your creditors.
- ❏ When your agent is ripping you off.

CBP is an opportunity to negotiate a lower fee for a star's performance, depending on how badly they need cash. But take note: performers hire gorillas to handle their CBP.

CASH ON DELIVERY

The purchaser pays cash on delivery (COD) of the goods. No credit is allowed. The cash is collected by the deliverer of the goods (before they are handed over) who deducts expenses and passes on the NET amount to the supplier. Alternatively, the deliverer pays the net amount to the supplier before delivery, and collects the GROSS amount on delivery.

CBP

See CASH BEFORE PERFORMANCE.

CHILDREN

The world's best negotiators.

Children:

- know how to get what they want;
- are utterly ruthless at having their needs met;
- have no sense of responsibility;
- have no sense of shame or feelings of remorse or notion of guilt;
- have no milk of human kindness;
- have no long-term plans.

Parents:

- give in to their children;
- give in to each other;
- are responsible;
- are easily shamed and in constant states of remorse;
- feel guilty (therefore they are guilty);
- are a fount of human kindness (and a bottomless pit for goodies);
- have long-term hopes (pensions, career, retirement, peace, "the best is yet to come").

Result: children win hands down.

They open negotiations on the balance between cabbage and ice cream with a firm refusal to eat any cabbage at all. You invariably start off by threatening "no cabbage, no ice cream". Your futile offers move through "some cabbage, then ice cream", to "just look at the cabbage for a second, and you can have the ice cream". Finally, you give in and pass the ice cream.

The children's strengths are their determination to meet high ASPIRATIONS, to use emotional BLACKMAIL and to live for their immediate gratification.

But parents have the last laugh because children grow up and acquire a taste for things that can only be got by negotiation (what is courtship but an early attempt at negotiation?). In short, they become conditioned like the rest of us. We win.

CIRCUMSTANCES

"Broken noses alter faces, circumstances alter cases" is the negotiator's litany when faced with an ambiguous case. The law tries to be tidy. Human relationships create new cases in new circumstances for which the drafters of the rules never planned.

Negotiators establish that the circumstances are unique and that the ordinary rules do not apply. Whether you agree depends on their plausibility, the genuineness of the different circumstances and the relative inevitability of the precedent being set.

COALITION

Negotiations are often between coalitions. First you negotiate within your coalition. Their particular INTERESTS may not correspond completely with yours.

Here are some basic rules.

☐ If you cannot convince your partners of the stance you intend to take, review your chances of convincing others.

☐ Take a COMMAND DECISION if your PREPARATION time is taken up with total disagreement between you and your partners.

☐ Avoid negotiating with more than one STRATEGY, or views on tradable concessions, and "leaders" with differing views about negotiable ranges.

Disarray in another coalition is usually a result of a dispute about their negotiating objectives, one lot preferring an accommodation with your view (the moderates), the other demanding a tougher line (the militants).

Take advantage of these divisions to achieve your objectives by assisting the moderate position to prevail, not by crushing the entire coalition.

☐ Support the ideas, not the personalities, of the moderates closest to your position

☐ If the moderates are the majority of the coalition, propose accommodating moves to isolate the militants.

❏ If the moderates are in a minority, demonstrate that the pay-off for being militant is less than the pay-off for being moderate.

How not to take advantage:

❏ By pointedly preferring the moderates.
❏ By mocking their coalition's disarray.
❏ By personalising their differences.
❏ By toughening your demands to the extent that you reunite the coalition.
❏ By rewarding or encouraging militancy.

Caution: Be aware that the militant–moderate "disarray" may be a TOUGH GUY/NICE GUY ploy.

COD
See CASH ON DELIVERY.

COERCION
Facing a conflict of INTERESTS, you can coerce your opponent into capitulation.

Coercion can be a two-way process: each side attempts to coerce the other with threats or with violent or expensive actions. You risk having to implement your threats and suffer the costs of the consequences. Law courts, strikes and wars are expensive.

Remember:

• Negotiation is rational if there are high risks of damaging hostilities.
• Coercion is appropriate if there are serious risks of conceding "too much".

Coercion is a COMMITMENT PLOY to do something unpleasant unless your opponents comply. If they comply you win, they lose (the Cuban missiles crisis). They can also counter-commit, forcing you to do what you threatened. Fear of the high costs of failure drive you both into negotiating stances.

To back off from coercion:

- ❏ Reduce the imminence of your threats.
- ❏ Extend to vague deadlines.
- ❏ Minimise outright provocation.

Peace can still fall apart with one miscalculated move.

COLLATERAL

Almost anything that the lender will accept as cover for the RISK of lending you money is collateral. For example, the lender holds one part and you keep the other, such as high value notes, or bearer bonds.

Borrowers arrange a loan against an item of greater value than the loan. If you default on the loan, the lender makes a profit by selling their collateral.

To act as collateral the item must be of sufficient value:

- to encourage your repayment of the loan;
- to cover the lender's loss if you do not.

Your risks in accepting items as collateral include the possibility that the borrower does not own them.

COLLECTIVE BARGAINING

Jointly determined rules for the use of labour in employment.

The rules are negotiated by unions either directly with an employer or with an AGENT of the employer and cover:

- remuneration;
- hours of work;
- types of work;
- performance standards;
- holidays;
- other entitlements;
- flexibility;
- restrictions;

- lay-offs;
- standards;
- work rates;
- overtime;
- retirement provisions;
- promotion;
- responsibilities and obligations of the bargaining agents;
- relationships between the bargaining agents;
- definitions of reasonable conduct;
- disciplinary procedures;
- procedures for resolving disputes.

There are efficiency benefits to management in having collective agreements with bargaining agents representing employees because individual negotiations could produce different rules for each employee. There are costs too. The bargaining agent:

- interferes with managerial independence;
- urges employees to show loyalty to, and accept discipline from, the union;
- can initiate disruption in the company;
- can introduce a division within a company which cuts across, or threatens, a company culture based on excellence, pride, self-respect and mutual goal-seeking.

Should you join a union?

☐ No, if the relative gains from bargaining for yourself exceed those of hiring somebody else to do it for you.

☐ Yes, if the agent has the superior detailed expertise (they deal with similar issues every day).

☐ No, if the union concentrates its effort on modest gains for the collective, rather than larger gains for the individual.

COMMAND DECISION

When a negotiating team cannot agree on a tactic or style appropriate to the circumstances, or cannot agree on the contents of an OFFER, the most

senior negotiator can make a command decision
by virtue of rank alone. The decision carries its
own authority and the team falls into line. Command decisions are not necessarily correct decisions, but the wrong decision may be better than
no decision and, as the person making it takes
full responsibility, reckless use of a commander's
privileges carries penalties.

COMMISSION
Payment for services rendered, for exceeding
sales targets, for introducing clients, and so on
(see BRIBERY).

Because the GROSS value of an income stream is
always larger than the NET value:

- propose that your commission is a percentage of gross rather than net value;
- offer them commission as a percentage of
  net rather than gross value.

Gross values keep the negotiator honest. Net
value is open to ambiguity.

- Net of what?
- Who decides the deductibles?

Avoid statements offering you percentages of
their "earnings from the contract that directly arise
from your efforts".

- "Earnings" after their accountants have had a
  go will not amount to much.
- "Directly arises" confines you to quibbles
  about how much you did and how much
  they had to do after you set it up.

COMMITMENT PLOY
Methods to make a THREAT credible. For example,
unless they comply with your demand you can
bind yourself to an irrevocable course of action
that would do immense damage to them irrespective of what damage it does to you. The more
certain your commitment (you die too) the more

credible your threat, and the more likely they will comply.

To apply commitment:

❏ Make known your commitment.
❏ Show that you mean what you say.

Dire warnings from them of the consequences of your commitment (plant closures, job losses, long strikes, war, and so on) reinforce the impact of your commitment ("this negotiator is irrational, I had better be more careful").

Undermine their commitment using SALAMI ploys. A specific threat to boycott, STRIKE, launch a thermonuclear war, unless you comply, is vulnerable to minute challenges.

- They demand a meeting by April 10th, you offer one on April 11th.
- They demand progress to reform in six months, you schedule talks about it for eight months (then query the details of arrangements).
- They demand no more than 10% penetration of their markets by your EXPORTS, you send 10.43%.

Salami counters undermine commitment, because the THREAT is disproportionate to the challenge. By carefully extending the challenge in size and number you widen the credibility gap between their commitment and their behaviour.

COMMUNICATION
Messages are misunderstood, misinterpreted and mislaid.

- The message sent need not be the one that is received.
- They may entirely miss the significance of your message.
- They need not believe what you are saying.
- They could doubt the provenance of the message.

- Your message does not make sense to them.

Threats, promises and commitments have little effect if they cannot be communicated.

We communicate by what we say, how we say it and our body language. The latter accounts for a greater proportion of the message received than the other two together. If our gestures say something different from our speech, and this is perceived by the receiver, we have a credibility problem.

A written communication can be re-read many times.

- It has the benefit of permanence.
- It has the drawback of inflexibility.
- It does not score highly on subtlety and nuance.

This is why others react negatively to what they perceive to be your written insults, callousness, abruptness and threats, particularly in the difficult phase of a negotiation where the parties are debating the issues closely.

Use the telephone to bolster your firmness. It is easier to say no on the telephone than to say it face to face. Use the fax to make enquiries, quote first offers and confirm agreement (it is not so good for negotiating complex proposals).

COMPETITIVE STYLE
Competitive negotiators try to win at any cost, which is why they lose. The competitive style is abrasive. The other negotiator is an enemy, not an ally. Anything he or she gets is at your expense. It is total war and ZERO SUM.

COMPROMISE
Compromise produces a solution short of CAPITU-LATION.

CONCESSION
Never concede anything: TRADE.

CONCESSION DILEMMA

Consider the gap between the current offers of two negotiators. You are constrained by a desire not to concede everything. You are in conflict with the other negotiator as to the extent of your mutual concessions. You aim to do better than CAPITULATION. Questions with uncertain answers include the following.

- How far must you move?
- How far will they move?
- Is their refusal a genuine inability to agree to your present terms or are they testing your resolve?

From the other side's point of view:

- Your last OFFER could have been your final offer but they have no way of knowing what is in your mind.
- Should they respond to your increasing resistance to moving further by moving towards a settlement, or should they continue to press for more movement?
- Is your last offer a prelude to increased resistance or to your capitulation?

CONCESSION RATE

Negotiators who move quickly at first and then stop are likely to frustrate other negotiators because:

- the early movement created EXPECTATIONS;
- the later non-movement frustrated them.

Negotiators who move slowly at first and then quickly are likely to harden the stance of other negotiators because the quicker movement signals that a hard line produces results.

Negotiators who sometimes move quickly and sometimes slowly provoke pressure from other negotiators because they do not know how to get movement, so they apply pressure.

Negotiators who move slowly do better

because their consistency is predictable. and if they only move in response to a TRADE they also signal how to get movement.

CONCESSION SIGNAL

Negotiators who have a reputation for hardly moving once they make their proposals induce other negotiators to attempt to delay them opening until their proposals have been influenced.

Negotiators who move in diminishing steps, starting with relatively large concessions and ending with smaller and smaller concessions signal that an exit PRICE is being approached.

Negotiators who move unpredictably, sometimes offering a large concession followed by a small one and sometimes the reverse, induce other negotiators to look for large concessions each time and to be disappointed if they are not forthcoming.

CONCILIATION

Alternative form of dispute resolution (see MEDIATION) to reconcile the parties in dispute, not to judge between them. Useful in fractious cases where the normal relationship between the parties has broken down.

CONDITIONAL LANGUAGE

States the negotiator's terms for settling an issue. "Give me some of what I want, and I will give you some of what you want."

Effective negotiators use conditional language when making an OFFER.

- On condition that . . .
- Provided that . . .
- If you will do such and such, then I will agree to do so and so.

Conditional language educates the other negotiator in how the issue can be settled.

CONFLICT

A reason for negotiating.

We cannot negotiate a variance a views, beliefs, attitudes, INTERESTS, actions, desires, needs, ASPIRATIONS, intentions, hopes, dispositions, EXPECTATIONS, principles and values but we can negotiate the practical applications of them and the competition for a scarce resource, be it tangible or intangible.

Irreconcilable conflicts are resolved by "live and let live" or the outright triumph of one side. The decision is "peace or war?"

Reconcilable conflicts are resolved by PERSUASION, PROBLEM-SOLVING, MEDIATION, ARBITRATION or negotiation. The decision is "debate or TRADE?"

CONFLICT OF INTERESTS AND RIGHTS

When parties have differing notions about their relationship, or the terms of doing business together, they have a conflict of interests. When parties dispute the application of an agreed PROCEDURE, such as in a disciplinary case, they have a conflict of rights.

"INTERESTS" and "rights" are common terminology in COLLECTIVE BARGAINING to distinguish how the conflict is to be resolved, whether within the terms of existing procedures (conflict of rights), including reinterpretation of clauses (through a judicial or quasi-judicial process), or through fresh negotiations to create a new AGREEMENT (conflict of interests).

US terminology distinguishes between a "contractual dispute" (one involving differing perceptions of "rights") and a "terminal dispute" (one involving differing perceptions of a future relationship when the parties are out of contract). French terminology distinguishes between *conflits juridiques* and *conflits économiques*.

CONSTANT

What is non-negotiable, whether by convention, custom and practice, lethargy, ignorance, convenience, or precedent. Contrast with TRADABLES.

Identify the constants in your business. What benefits are there in having non-tradable constants? Who determined that they are non-tradable?

Examples of constants could include:

- scale fees;
- minimum rental periods;
- minimum stock levels;
- minimum order quantities;
- credit terms;
- use of in-house services;
- purchase of own company products;
- compulsory insurance;
- exclusive dealing through specified agents;
- single sourced suppliers.

Consider the advantages gained from changing constants into tradables.

CONSTANT SUM

Jargon from GAME THEORY. Where the sum of the pay-offs to the negotiators remains the same across all possible solutions to the dispute (see ZERO SUM).

CONSULTING FEE

Why do some consultants make more money than others? Because many consultants do not appreciate why they are being consulted.

Consultants are hired for their expertise, yet most of them sell their time instead of their expertise. Time costs less than expertise. A consultant's expertise is only valuable because it saves the time and expense of acquiring it ourselves.

Many experts think in terms of what it legitimately costs them to provide the advice. The formula is: divide annual GROSS salary costs by the number of available working days, add a margin for administrative costs and a margin for profit and charge out services at a daily rate.

The alternative method is to charge a percentage of the gross value of your advice to the client.

CONTINGENCY PRICING

A method of pricing an uncertain value.

Valuations of the future worth of a business are

as variable as the parties' INTERESTS. Buyers understate future worth, sellers exaggerate it. To set the PRICE for the business offer a basic price which is less than the seller is demanding, plus an amount contingent on whether the future conforms to the seller's opinion or to the buyer's.

- Buyer's downside. The future is a result of the buyer's beneficial contribution, and not just the intrinsic worth of future business.
- Seller's downside. The buyer controls the business and can influence its future performance to understate its true worth.

CONTRACT LAW

A highly technical subject monopolised by lawyers. The advice offered here is a common sense summary of the main principles, which inevitably apply differently in each country. (Check with your lawyer in your own INTERESTS, but pay for his or her time not expertise.)

A contract determines the terms under which a business or personal relationship is conducted. It is enforceable at law (though enforceability varies in different countries).

Generally an OFFER to contract is valid if the parties communicate their intentions to be under contract to one another and if the bargain is specified (that is, there is a consideration). If an offer is unconditionally accepted, there is an enforceable contract (providing the subject of the contract is not illegal). An offer lapses if acceptance is unduly delayed and can be withdrawn on communicating this to the other party before they accept.

An offer to contract is accepted if the acceptance is unconditional, is communicated to the offeror by the named offeree and does not amend the offered contract.

A contract is valid unless you can prove duress, fraud, illegality, or undue influence.

Contracts consist of six main elements.

1 The identity and location of the contracting parties.

2   What they are contracting to do.
3   What their rewards are for performing the contract.
4   What the penalties are for non-performance.
5   Duration, legal basis, reversion and revision rules.
6   Confirmed signatures of the parties.

CO-OPERATIVE STYLE

Negotiators are co-operative antagonists.

Your antagonisms arise from your conflicting, or competing, goals; your co-operation arises when DEADLOCK leaves you both worse off than COMPROMISE.

COPYRIGHT

Do not sell it for a mess of pottage.

Copyright in a book, a play, or any creative script lasts for your lifetime plus 50 years. Your estate earns ROYALTIES after death. After a copyright lapses anybody can publish your work without paying royalties.

❑ Insist on retaining your copyright.

❑ Licence the publisher to exploit your work for a royalty for a limited duration of 5–10 years.

❑ Do not give it authority to assign your licence to third parties.

❑ Insist that if it fails to meet the terms of the contract or goes bankrupt, the licence unconditionally reverts to you.

❑ Do not let liquidators of publishers treat your copyright as a forfeited asset.

CORRUPTION

No way to do business, but in many places the only way to get into, and around, some countries just to look for business, or simply to stay out of trouble (see BRIBERY).

If you are "on the take" examine your vulnerabilities: the briber has a row with her lover, he shops you both in revenge; the briber gets caught, and confesses about you in exchange for a shorter sentence; you fall out with your lover, she exacts her revenge; you get caught. . .

COST BREAKDOWN

Worth getting if it identifies the TRADABLES and the PADDING. Volunteering one is not so hot; it gives the other side ideas.

To get a detailed breakdown show a written policy from your organisation requiring a breakdown before an order is placed.

To resist supplying a breakdown:

- Show a written policy prohibiting your organisation, or yourself, from doing so.
- Claim that "proprietary information", and so on, is at stake.
- Refer the buyer to your competitors' prices, and assert that this is the deciding factor, not how you go about your business.

COUNTER-TRADE

A complex form of barter which can take several forms.

- **Counter-purchase.** The parties agree to a linked protocol to purchase equivalent amounts of goods from each other using foreign currency.
- **Buy-back.** The provider buys back the output of a plant it provides to the other country.
- **Bilateral clearing.** The parties export goods, paid in local currencies, which are credited against an agreed total.
- OFF-SET. The buyer is compensated for a purchase by the seller agreeing to purchase goods to an agreed value from the buyer country.

Traders without hard currency can exchange goods instead. The financing is done locally for each party under their own arrangements. The practice is common where trade finance is weak or the political risks are high.

The goods offered for counter-trade are unconnected to the goods supplied. When the goods have obvious commercial value ask: Why don't they sell the goods themselves and pay me from the proceeds? If you do not want to counter-trade, say no firmly and repeatedly.

The goods are not always of obvious value. Sellers pad the value of the goods they offer, so challenge whatever PRICE they put on them. It is not the counter-trader's "price" but the selling price (NET of transport, insurance, RISK and marketing) of the goods in your own or a third country that counts.

If they spring a counter-trade deal on you after a money price has been agreed for some goods you plan to sell to them they could be bluffing to finesse additional discounts from you; it is only a device to lower your money price.

COURTESY
Nobody ever got a worse deal by being courteous.

CREDIT
Give it, and pay it when due.

CREDIT CONTROL
It is easier to avoid debts than to collect them.

- ☐ Know who owes you money.
- ☐ Require them to establish their creditworthiness.
- ☐ Set pre-determined limits on amounts allowed to be outstanding.
- ☐ State the days allowed to be overdue.
- ☐ State the time allowed to pay.
- ☐ Set rates of repayment.
- ☐ Seek COLLATERAL for the loan.

If you are running into repayment problems inform your creditors early because they TRUST debtors who talk to them in advance marginally more than those who are evasive. An unexplained debt excites suspicions and receives most of the energetic attention of credit controllers.

When renegotiating a rescheduling of a debt your leverage increases with its size, for a large debt is a shared problem but a small one is yours alone.

CULTURE DIFFERENCES

They count. In a "foreign" country you are the foreigner. It is you that is the odd one out. Everything they do is perfectly natural where they live and work. You with your strange ways must adapt to them, not them to you, assuming you want to do business with them.

Take account of the differences, and accommodate to them where possible.

☐ If the Japanese pace of negotiation is slower than yours, then you had better slow down.

☐ If the American pace is faster, you had better speed up.

☐ If Arabs are not disciplined by TIME, then allow for it when negotiating with them.

☐ If Russians are suspicious, do not behave suspiciously.

☐ If the Chinese keep asking the same QUESTIONS and do not appear to take no for an answer, answer patiently with variations on how to say no.

In short, abide by the advice to travellers going to Rome.

DEADLINES

Can help or hinder, depending on who discloses that they have one.

Deadlines put you under pressure. But this pressure is as nothing compared with the pressure you attract if you disclose your deadlines to the other negotiators.

Will they take advantage of your predicament? Yes. It stiffens their resolve not to move towards you; they know that you will soon be leaping towards them. Hence, do not disclose deadlines that the other negotiators have no other means of knowing about.

Deadlines that help you are those that:

- force the other negotiators to decide;
- the other negotiators disclose;
- the other negotiators do not control;
- impose costs on the others;
- give you options;
- you control;
- they know you will stick by.

Deadlines that hinder you are those that:

- are arbitrary;
- are imposed by your own people;
- they know about;
- are imminent;
- remove your discretion;
- cannot be ignored.

DEADLOCK

We negotiate because we face the deadlock of disagreement. Unblocking deadlock could be a victory for good sense, or of bad judgment. It depends on whether and what we TRADE to get an AGREEMENT. Many companies go bust because they negotiate unprofitable agreements, not because they cannot find enough customers.

If the most the buyer offers is less than the least the seller will accept, deadlock is inevitable, unless one or both change their exit PRICE.

Single issue BARGAINING is more prone to

deadlock: you resist conceding when you get nothing back (ZERO SUM). Widen the issues, increase the AGENDA, be creative with the PACKAGING of the tradable variables.

Deadlocked on price?

☐ Pay in some other way.
☐ Pay less now, more later.
☐ Pay more now, less later.
☐ Pay some in cash, the rest in kind.
☐ Pay in another currency in another country.
☐ Split the invoice across different budgets.

Deadlocked on a single issue?

☐ Compensate by movement on another issue.
☐ Link several issues together.
☐ Set the issue aside while settling the other issues.

Deadlocked on the value of future trade?

☐ Apply CONTINGENCY PRICING: if your estimate materialises, your PRICE applies; if theirs materialises, their price applies.

Deadlocked across the issues?

☐ Amend the specification (what are marginal changes in performance worth?)
☐ Alter the TIME structure of events (SALAMI?)
☐ Change the responsibilities (who delivers? who inspects? who insures? who secures? who warrants? who risks? who owns?)
☐ Change the nature of the business (from production to distribution; from home-made to importing; from foreign to local ownership; from ownership to management; from management to ROYALTIES; from royalties to buy-out).

Deadlock ploys play on negotiators' FEAR OF DEADLOCK. If they "fail" to agree, they anticipate pressures from the people behind them. Hence, they move rather than lose.

To threaten deadlock:

☐ Talk up the difficulties of reaching an AGREEMENT.

☐ Introduce phoney deadlines.

☐ Stage phoney walk-outs.

☐ Exhibit phoney temper.

☐ Become unavailable.

☐ Demonstrate pessimism.

☐ Accuse them of not wanting an agreement.

☐ Make "final offers".

Counter: Show no fear of deadlock.

DEBT COLLECTING

Not for the squeamish, the gullible or the saintly. A bad debt is like theft, except you know the name of the thief.

- Some people do not pay and never intended to pay.
- Some people intended to pay but find it convenient not to pay.
- Some people do not pay because they cannot pay.
- Some people only pay if you make them pay.

Letters and phone calls are useful to a point, but hard-nosed debtors develop plausible imaginations.

- The cheque is in the post.
- I am in conference with my accountant and will ring you back.
- Check with your bank, our cheque number was . . . dated the . . . of last month.

Counters: What leverage do you have? Can you run up debts using their services to the value of the money they owe you? When they try to collect, reveal the NET balance and call it quits.

Collecting debts is best done in person. Invariably you can collect something towards payment (do not be snowed with a promise).

No debt is ever a matter of principle. If you find yourself believing that it is, consider: how much can you make while you are tied up with an obsession about principles?

Remember any payment is better than none, including in kind.

DEBT SWAMP

Swamps are not just messy, they can kill you.

A debt swamp has an inevitability about it. The more you struggle the deeper you sink.

In the debt swamp you borrow money for a purchase (a house, a car, a yacht). These have costs (taxes, repairs, maintenance, and so on) as does the loan (interest and principal). If the costs of the loan total more than your income, you get your feet wet in the swamp.

If you have insufficient income you can borrow the difference and get more than your feet wet. As the debt swamp rises, your insufficient income is squeezed. In desperation you turn to a lender and borrow to keep the swamp down; but borrowing more puts you further into the swamp.

DECISION ANALYSIS

A negotiator's PREPARATION tool.

To choose a course of action (whether to or not, whether to go in high or low, whether to take what is on or not, and so on), estimate the value of the competing outcomes and their probability of being realised.

Estimate the probabilities on the basis of experience. Broadly, choosing an action with a very high value may mean simultaneously reducing the probability of achieving it. Increasing the probability of success by making it more likely to be acceptable means reducing the expected value of the outcome.

Each outcome is given a value V and a probability p of its occurring. $V \times p = EV$ gives its expected value.

Set a minimum expected value to assess the probable outcomes against and calculate the expected values of each option.

For example, if the value of the contract is $200 and your estimate of the probability of being successful is 60%, then the expected value of the outcome is $200 x 0.6 = $120. But you have negotiating costs too, and the probability of your proposal being unsuccessful is $1 - 0.6 = 0.4$.

The expected value to you of being unsuccessful is your negotiating cost (say, $20) times the probability of this event occurring: $20 x 0.4 = $8. Now the expected value of negotiating for the contract is the sum of the expected values of each event: $120 - 8 = $112. If this is higher than your minimum expected value, negotiate for the contract; if lower, do not.

The analysis can be extended to cover more complex decisions, although the principle is the same.

DELAYING PLOY

Time changes the balance of POWER and we need ploys to avoid a decision.

Take two belligerents considering the future of their war. They should sue for peace when there is a stalemate. But the fortunes of war wax and wane. Negotiations are unlikely while each side has different opinions of their fortunes.

Consider a war where each side recognises that continued conflict is unproductive. Suppose peace negotiations begin. What do the negotiators do if there is an unexpected military reverse for one of the parties? At the very least, the winning side has a strong incentive to slow down the negotiations, for each day's delay strengthens their BARGAINING power.

Delaying ploys include:

- quibbling about details;
- taking longer adjournments;
- seeking further instructions;
- "diplomatic" illness;
- abiding by national holidays;
- provoking rows;

- feigning insults;
- changing the delegation;
- raising old issues;
- insisting on full translations;
- requesting venue changes;
- cancelling meetings;
- starting late;
- finishing early.

Similar ploys can be used in strikes which swing one way and the other.

DELIVERY
Charge for it as an ADD-ON; demand it as a DISCOUNT.

DEVIL'S ADVOCATE
A PREPARATION tool. A negotiator takes the role of expressing directly contrary positions to the ones prepared by the team. This tests your arguments for soundness and consistency.

Thinking through your proposed responses to the arguments advanced by the devil's advocate tests their credibility and exposes deficiencies in the data or preparation, which allows you time to fill in the gaps.

DICKER
American for HAGGLE.

DISCOUNT
A deduction from a PRICE.

Discounts are given for all kinds of reasons. Some are common in particular businesses and have a habit of growing into permanent features of an invoicing system because they set precedents.

An invoice is discounted to:

- encourage payment on time;
- order large volumes;
- pay in advance;
- pay something on an overdue account;
- maintain loyalty;
- place an order before a set date, and so on.

After the event, the client expects the discount to continue. Rival suppliers respond to price discounting by offering discounts themselves. The result is a PRICE WAR.

Negotiators should always ask for discounts, and should be creative about the reasons they require them. Discounts can be demanded credibly for:

- ☐ Early payment.
- ☐ Advance payment.
- ☐ Payment of a deposit.
- ☐ Large volume.
- ☐ Purchase of several items.
- ☐ The right to use your name in supplier advertising.
- ☐ End of stock purchase.
- ☐ First of stock purchase.
- ☐ Reward for recommending supplier to other customers.
- ☐ Loyalty to supplier over the years.
- ☐ First time use of supplier.
- ☐ Placing all your business with supplier.
- ☐ Placing some of your business on introductory basis.
- ☐ Seasonal purchases.
- ☐ Delivery at awkward times.
- ☐ Rescheduled deliveries.
- ☐ Instant delivery.
- ☐ Delayed delivery.
- ☐ Collecting from supplier ex-works with own transport.
- ☐ Missed delivery.
- ☐ Incomplete or mistaken order.
- ☐ Any inconvenience caused by supplier, and so on.

DISTRIBUTIVE BARGAINING

Examples of distributive bargaining include the following.

- A wage rise which increases employees' incomes and employer's costs.
- A PRICE negotiation which benefits the buyer and reduces the income of the seller.

- A boundary or territorial negotiation by which one country reduces the territory of another.

The algebraic sum of the gains and losses produce ZERO SUM outcomes (see also INTEGRATIVE BARGAINING).

If we divide a scarce resource between us, what you gain I lose. However, conflict is not unbounded. Neither of us can get our own way entirely (if we could we would not bother negotiating).

Do not negotiate when you are:

- in a hurry;
- exhausted;
- emotionally involved;
- sexually aroused;
- busy with other tasks;
- late for an appointment;
- bored;
- angry;
- under pressure;
- meant to be elsewhere;
- desperate;
- under the influence of drink or drugs;
- euphoric;
- suspicious;
- jet-lagged;
- hungry;
- in need of a visit to the rest room.

DRIPPING ROAST

Sweat once, benefit many times. Win an order and bask in the income from the repeat business.

Dripping roasts are sound business, if you can get them. Your small percentage turns over regularly, for no additional effort. Do not knock the small dripping roasts: they pay the rent.

DUTCH AUCTION

If you have two or more bids for the same item, instead of selling to the highest or buying from the lowest bidder, contact each bidder separately and offer them an opportunity to improve on their rival's last BID. This is mistakenly called a "Dutch auction".

Keen buyers re-bid just above their rivals, and keen sellers cut their prices to just below their rivals, in the hope of winning. Try several rounds of quoting and re-quoting the last bid to the rivals (and why not if the bidders want to keep bidding?) until only one bidder survives.

EMOTION

Used sparingly, emotion can help a negotiator express commitment.

There are emotional traps in:

- sending messages;
- signalling EXPECTATIONS;
- underlining a THREAT or PROMISE;
- establishing RAPPORT;
- overcoming obstacles;
- reinforcing TRUST;
- altering PERCEPTION.

CONFLICT generates emotions and can be an obstacle to progress; it can inhibit judgment of self-interest; it can protract a negotiation and provoke DEADLOCK.

Reduce emotional tension by:

☐ Refraining from exciting INHIBITIONS.

☐ Refraining from mocking their weaknesses or setbacks.

☐ Demonstrating willingness to understand, if not to agree with, their views and INTERESTS.

☐ Refraining from emotional attacks.

☐ Refraining from challenging their motives, integrity and legitimacy.

Faced with an emotional outburst, either in attack or defence, remain calm. Emotion dies down more quickly if it is not fed.

It is difficult to eliminate emotions when you have strong feelings for or against the other negotiator for some reason (family, friendship, love, sympathy, likeability, solidarity, suspicion, distrust, previous "dirty tricks", duplicity, unfulfilled promises, and such like). But deals led by emotions, positive or negative, are worse deals than those that you remain clear-headed about.

ESCALATION

A measured pressure ploy, sometimes used unethically. Jumping from peace to all-out war is unusual. First, a little pressure is applied, then some more, and eventually full pressure is imposed.

If DEADLOCK is caused by their unreasonable obstinacy, the escalation might work. On the other hand, their "obstinacy" might be due to your unreasonable demands, as they perceive them. Your escalating pressure only convinces them that you are being unreasonable. You risk a mixture of indignation and MARTYRDOM, which results in stiffening resistance rather than surrender.

ESCALATOR SCHEDULE

A formula to increase an agreed share in uncertain future income streams.

Publishers normally agree to escalate an author's percentage ROYALTIES as sales reach specified quantities. Similarly, anybody owning rights to a product should negotiate escalator clauses in their licensing agreements.

Tactically, your aim is to increase the percentage royalty or fee and decrease the qualifying amount which triggers off the increased royalty (and in reverse if you are acquiring the licence).

If negotiating COMMISSION terms (or performance-related pay), go for an escalator clause: so much for reaching a performance level and extra amounts for exceeding it.

It is better to negotiate this before improving performance, as trying to do so later is vulnerable to the HOOKER'S PRINCIPLE.

ETHICS

Do not preach to others about your ethics if you want to influence them. There is not a lot to choose between the unethical and the sanctimonious.

You should take account of potential costs from unethical conduct, including the attention of the law, public contempt and damage to your reputation.

EXCHANGE

How decisions are made by negotiation. You exchange things you have for things you want;

you exchange your consent for a consideration;
you exchange something you value for peace.

EXPECTATIONS

You have them: they help determine your strategies and your objectives. If your expectations are
unrealisable, or you come to believe that they
are, you adjust them or pursue a hopeless quest
(see POWER).

EXPORTS

Without these we would all be poorer, yet everywhere otherwise sensible people seek to curb
each other's.

Exporting is complicated. Frontiers are jealously
guarded. Legal systems differ across the world
and disputes between people in separate territories
– with the goods, perhaps, in a third territory or in
transit between them – add to the normal com-
plexities (and costs). The number of intermedi-
aries involved in shipping goods imposes heavy
demands on comprehensive documentation, title
to ownership, transfer of ownership and timely
payment as agreed between seller and buyer.

At a minimum documentation is required to
describe the goods, to value them and to authen-
ticate the declaration. The shipper (vessel, vehicle
or aircraft) has numerous formalities to complete
too. These formalities, and their associated costs,
incline the prudent seller towards an ex-works
PRICE for the goods, leaving the hassle of exporting to the buyer.

EXPORT CREDIT

World trade must be financed by credit to the buyer
and, also, credit to the seller waiting for payment.

Your options for ensuring payment include the
following.

• **Cash with order:** if you can get it.
• **Documentary credit.** Payment on presentation of shipping documents to buyer's bank (insist
that the credit is "irrevocable", and "confirmed" so
that you can receive payment at your local bank).

• **Transferable credit.** When you are selling as an AGENT. Your supplier wants payment when you order the goods for your buyer, but you do not get paid until the goods are shipped to the buyer. The solution is to arrange a documentary credit from your buyer in the normal way, but get its bank to pay your supplier its PRICE to you on proof of shipping the goods to you (this money is deducted from the documentary credit held in your name). When you ship the goods on to the buyer, you receive the balance of the credit on presentation of your shipping documents.

• **Back-to-back credit.** Use of the documentary credit in your favour from your buyer as security to establish a credit in your supplier's favour, paid when it ships the goods. Less favourable to you than a transferable credit.

• **Revolving credit.** For regular routine transactions that permit a cycle of credit to operate: as one transaction is paid on presentation of the appropriate documents, another is opened.

• **Acceptance credit.** A bank credits you with an amount which you can draw against and the bank places your bills in the money market; as the buyer's credits to you become due, these are collected by the bank to cover the acceptance allowed to you on the strength of your transaction with the buyer.

You can use your EXPECTATIONS of getting paid by a buyer (the credit system you negotiate) to raise finance. The credit is an asset, albeit a paper one. You can sell the credit for a discounted price, the purchaser collecting the difference as its GROSS profit when the documentary credit is paid. Your obligation to ship the goods remains; indeed, the purchaser of the bill can sue you (recourse) if you do not.

FACTORING

Invoices are bought by a factoring agency which collects payment from the buyers and pockets the difference between what it pays for the invoices and what it collects.

The factoring agency eliminates known bad payers, or potential bad payers, and requires a larger margin on some others. Some agencies use the supplier's own notepaper, so buyers are unaware they are dealing with a factor.

The spread between the factoring PRICE and the invoice's face value is negotiable as is whether the factor has recourse to the seller in the case of a bad debt.

FAILURE TO AGREE

A formal declaration required in COLLECTIVE BARGAINING procedure agreements when negotiators cannot settle the dispute at their level. Sometimes negotiators fail to agree on the "nod", so that an issue can reach an appropriate level more quickly.

FAIR

A sense of fairness influences negotiators (see NASH SOLUTION). If you were asked what you would regard as a fair distribution of a large sum of money between you and a colleague, and you were given no additional information, it is likely that you would prefer an "equal" distribution.

Fairness as a settlement option is popular with economists, because their negotiation models do not incorporate BARGAINING skills, POWER perceptions and EXPECTATIONS. By eliminating these the settlement must end up at the mid-point because there is no economic reason why it should end up anywhere else.

Fairness, however, is not a principle of nature, it is a construct of the mind.

FAIT ACCOMPLI

A ploy to shift POWER to the doer and raise the stakes if counter sanctions are applied.

Armies seize territory and then offer to negotiate;

a developer knocks down a unique building and then applies for planning permission; managers introduce new work schedules and then agree to negotiations; buyers send a cheque for a lesser amount than the disputed invoice; a buyer returns goods outside warranty and refuses to pay; a department occupies disputed office space and offers talks.

Counter: Write into your contract firm rules on what cannot be done without invoking heavy legal penalties.

FALL-BACK
If you have not got one, then you stand and fight where you are. Best to think about a fall-back if the negotiations do not work out as you expected. (See BATNA.)

FEAR OF DEADLOCK
Common enough in negotiation. The fear inhibits negotiators from standing firm, encourages GOOD-WILL concessions and opens them to exploitation. DEADLOCK implies "failure" and we do not like to fail. Much better for us to overcome the fear, and certainly never to disclose it.

FINAL OFFER
If you make one, mean it; otherwise do not. Final offers are risky and are foolhardy at the beginning of a negotiation. Final offers that become "final offers but one" (or two, or three) are disastrous for credibility. A "final offer" bluff, if called, is embarrassing.

To make final offers, pay attention to your language. If no more movement is possible – you are at your exit point and prefer no deal to one on worse terms – convey this. A badly phrased final offer, however, is a provocative ultimatum. Tell them:

- you can go "no further";
- you are at the "end of the road";
- that it is "decision time".

None of these statements mentions "final offer", but that is how it will be perceived.

Do not ask: Is that your final offer? The answer you get is not the one you want. They can hardly say no (the answer you want) without compromising their position, hence they are most likely to say yes, blocking off the negotiation.

FIRST OFFER

Never accept a first offer: negotiate.

The first offer is where they open; it is not where they expect to end up. If it is they are in such a powerful position that there is no need to negotiate.

If you accept their first offer, what other offers would you accept?

FIXED PRICE

Sellers love fixed prices because they preclude BARGAINING. That is why they write prices on large tickets, print price lists, have standard terms for doing business and imply that the price on the tag is fixed for good.

And why not? Most people accept fixed prices. Few challenge them, fewer still persist after the first no.

But the price on the tag, or printed on the list, is their FIRST OFFER. Whether it is their FINAL OFFER remains to be seen.

More often than not, the aversion to negotiating a better price has nothing to do with the buyer's relative POWER. It is part of the business culture you live in. 97% of people in the UK accept the buyer's first offer; in the USA it is down as low as 17% in some commodity groups; in Australia it is around 30%.

In business transactions, however, effective negotiators do not accept the price they are first quoted. They:

- HAGGLE;
- try to open up first offers to discussion;
- see what other offers are lurking in the background. (See DISCOUNT.)

FLEXIBILITY

In short supply among average negotiators. Flexibility in approach, not INTERESTS, comes from thorough PREPARATION. The above-average negotiator is armed with options, both as to goals and methods of achieving them.

FORCE MAJEURE

Events that are outside the control of the contracting parties which prevent a contractual obligation being met. Revolutions, war, seizure of assets, embargoes, economic sanctions, geological and climatic disturbances and suchlike can make fulfilment of a contract impossible, or severely delay completion. Include *force majeure* provisions in your contract.

FORCE PROJECTION

An indirect pressure ploy.

Unions use force projection in contract negotiations. They hold a mass march to be seen by the managers. A disturbance, a few arrests, TV coverage of a police baton charge or a fiery speech, all contribute to force projection (in this case, of determination).

Buyers' force projection measures include the following.

- Open contact with competition.
- Competitors' notepaper visible on desk.
- In-house costings in "make or buy?" report.
- Circular letter calling for tenders.

Sellers' force projection measures include the following.

- Surcharges on small orders.
- Lengthy delivery dates.
- Publicity about growing market share.
- Acquisition of, or merger with, rivals.

All force projection measures aim to influence the negotiators' EXPECTATIONS.

FORFAITING

Subject to certain conditions, a bank forfaits an invoice for an exporter by paying direct to the exporter an agreed proportion of its face value. The bank then assumes total responsibility for collecting the money from the importer, and usually does not have recourse to the exporter if its customer fails to pay.

The difference between the exporter's income from the bank and the face value of the invoice is justified by the certainty of payment compared with the usual risks faced by exporters. The terms of the forfaiting facility are negotiable.

FORMULA BARGAINING

An analytical approach to international diplomacy that divides negotiation into three phases:

- pre-negotiation or "diagnostic" phase;
- defining the appropriate "formula" phase;
- the "detail" phase.

Negotiators are advised to:

- pay attention to the facts, the history of the problem, and how it has evolved;
- look for precedents and how referents governing similar situations have developed;
- know about the specific contexts and perceptions of the disputants and how they perceive their INTERESTS.

The negotiators engage in a search for an agreed formula which refers to:

- an agreed definition of the conflict;
- cognitive referents that imply a solution;
- some criterion of justice.

Negotiators must "remember that the problem, not the other party, is the 'enemy' to be overcome".

The detail phase of the negotiations is a hard slog through the itemised applications of the formula.

Care is needed to:

- keep the "big picture" in focus while negotiating the details;
- be able to match flexibility with steadfastness in pursuit of clearly defined objectives;
- handle the "eyeball-to-eyeball" moments in major international negotiations where there is a knife-edge between success and resort to other options.

FRIENDSHIP

Neither necessary nor sufficient to get an AGREEMENT, but seldom a hindrance.

The personal relations of the negotiators can be warmer than the relations between the constituents they represent. This is not an uncommon experience in difficult (for example, peace treaty) negotiations.

Working on the interpersonal relationship can help, but in some contexts it can hinder. For example, negotiating with officials from a bureaucracy can lead to misunderstandings if your friendly gestures are thought to be enticing them into corrupt or disloyal stances. Certainly, if you are on good terms with the other side it is better than being hardly able to speak to them, but remember, the exploitation of the friendship is not all one way (they get to you too).

FRONTAL ASSAULT

A high-RISK ploy to COMPROMISE the other negotiator's credibility.

- That is not what your predecessor said to us last time we met.
- Perhaps you should adjourn and consult with your people in more detail before you dig in too deep on this issue?

The other negotiator is irritated by this ploy and may "blow his or her top". It could sour your relationship for good: use rarely.

GAME THEORY

Mathematical formulation of conflict dilemmas applied to the BARGAINING problem.

Game theory relies on key ASSUMPTIONS:

- the identity of the players and their number are fixed and known to everyone (you are not playing against the anonymous "market");
- all players are rational and everybody knows they are rational;
- the pay-offs to each player are known;
- each player's strategies are known and fixed.

The manipulation of available information for personal advantage between the players is limited, but not excluded, by the assumptions.

Two-person ZERO SUM games show that players in a pure conflict game assumed that the other person was malevolent and therefore disposed to "do his or her worst" whatever STRATEGY was selected. A player does best by selecting the strategy that assured the "best of the worst outcomes".

Two-person NON-ZERO SUM games are more complex. The degree of strategic interaction increases dramatically as they explore opportunities for mutual gain. (See NASH SOLUTION; PRISONER'S DILEMMA.)

GAZUMP

You think you have a contract. The other party considers it to be an intention. Somebody else offers them a better deal, so they drop their deal with you and sign a contract with them. You have been gazumped.

Gazumping can be inconvenient if you were relying on the transaction to go through.

Gazumping may be the only option you have if the other party is unable to close the deal within a reasonable period of time, or you need the deal more than you are concerned about the ETHICS of gazumping. Hence you gazump.

To avoid gazumping, negotiate an OPTION.

G

GENEROSITY

Not contagious without a high degree of TRUST between the negotiators. Making unconditional offers does not promote reciprocal GOODWILL. The other negotiators perceive you to be in a weaker position, and revise their initial demands accordingly.

Unless, and until, you develop a strong relationship with the other negotiator be like Scrooge rather than St Francis of Assisi.

GETTING OUT FROM UNDER

Deals go sour. If you are in the pit, stop digging; get out from under.

We hang on in the hope that something will turn up. To give up is a defeat, a sign of weakness, a confession of failure. Right? Wrong.

Digging in when we have clearly made a mistake is for dumbos.

If you cannot avoid the occasional lemon, get rid of it. After you have got out from under study why you got into the mess in the first place.

GETTING PAID

Not everybody gets paid what they are due. Getting paid is sometimes more difficult than doing the work you have not been paid for.

There can be genuine differences of opinion as to:

- how much is owed;
- what the agreed PRICE was;
- who was responsible for the revisions and variations;
- the quality of the completed work.

There are also failures to pay based on avoiding payment for wholly unscrupulous reasons.

Well-structured variation procedures identify the obligation to pay and disciplined invoicing systems collect your money. (See CREDIT CONTROL.)

GIVE AND TAKE

A description of the negotiator's trading behaviour. A caveat:

- "giving" does not cause "getting";
- "taking" does not cause "giving".

Trading requires linked give and take – one goes with the other – and therefore only offer to give if you simultaneously get something back in exchange.

GO-BETWEEN

Trade name for someone akin to an AGENT, particularly in the Middle East.

A go-between is usually a national of the importing country who acts as the contact person between you and the importer. It is not always clear exactly who the go-between acts for but several countries insist that foreigners do all their business through a local one. In exchange for handling the transactions between the parties, the go-between receives a COMMISSION paid by the foreigner out of his or her share of the transaction.

As go-betweens often also act for the other party, or at least are candid with him or her about your limits, they can hardly be described as bona fide agents. Their status is inescapably ambiguous. Casual recruitment of a go-between can prove expensive. Consult your embassy's commercial attaché before embarking on a contract with a go-between.

GOODWILL

Earned but not given automatically.

Conceding something, no matter how little, in order to "create goodwill" is futile. The other negotiators stiffen their position when you make unconditional offers. Also, the "little" things you give away may acquire considerable leverage potential later in the negotiation – they could even clinch the AGREEMENT if offered at the right time – and throwing them away in the futile hope of creating goodwill is extremely costly when the result is that you have nothing left to close the deal.

GREED

Snatching DEADLOCK out of the jaws of COMPROMISE by being too greedy.

G

You do not intend to be greedy, only ambitious. The other negotiator resents your greed and resists. You end up with nothing.

GRIEVANCE

Do not just state a grievance, propose a remedy.

Concentrate your attention on your grievance and you are likely to argue. Think about what you want done about your grievance, and select a proportionate remedy within the other negotiator's gift (beware of GREED), and you are likely to enjoy the remedy sooner than you will settle an ARGUMENT.

GROSS

The gross of anything is larger than the NET.

A percentage of gross income is worth more than a percentage of gross profit, and both are worth more than a percentage of net income or net profit respectively. Especially true when the other negotiator controls the calculation of the net.

GUARANTEE

Of great value where the risks of non-compliance are high. Banks take guarantees to cover their loans; clients want guarantees to cover your performance (see PERFORMANCE BOND); you like guarantees when it's your money at stake.

- ❏ Make sure, when giving guarantees, that you can pay up if things go wrong ("Murphy's Law" is no joke).
- ❏ Extravagant guarantees are dangerous.
- ❏ Ask for guarantees.
- ❏ If they cannot guarantee something, adjust the PRICE downwards.
- ❏ If they guarantee something as a matter of course, ask for a price without the guarantee (you are paying for it in an insurance premium anyway).
- ❏ If the guarantee needs to be invoked, consider a payment in lieu of litigation to collect it.

HAGGLE

A noble art. The seller discovers the maximum a buyer will pay, without disclosing the minimum he or she will accept (and vice versa).

Haggling is part theatre. Effective hagglers:

- give plausible reasons for you to improve your OFFER;
- rely on sympathy, emotions, their "facts" and your lack of stamina;
- use mutual convergence between their and your current prices to secure an AGREEMENT;
- use silence effectively while waiting for you to move;
- enter high/low to create room to move more slowly in smaller steps towards you than you move in larger steps towards them.

HAVING IT BOTH WAYS

Negotiators often do, if you let them. For example, an increase in rent of \$100 is an "intolerable burden"; an OFFER of \$100 as a pay increase is an "insult".

Counter: Draw attention to the inconsistency; but negotiators believe what they want to believe.

HEADS OF AGENDA

A useful device to get stalled talks restarted.

Your differences with the other side could be sharp. You find it impossible to:

- handle all the differences;
- decide which issues should be tackled first;
- choose which issues should be tackled at all;
- separate out the poisoned relations between the parties.

Try for a heads of agenda which does not contain proposals and requires no explanation. Agree a set of headings of the issues you want to discuss. These need not be placed in any particular order. If you can agree on even a restricted list of headings, this could precipitate enough momentum to allow the negotiations to recommence.

HEADS OF AGREEMENT
Device for reaching basic agreement on the broad issues before settling the contractual details. Much used in property negotiations.

HOOKER'S PRINCIPLE
Services are valued more highly before they are performed than they are afterwards. When, for instance, does a plumber's fee look reasonable? When you are up to your knees in water.

Always agree the basis under which you expect to be paid before you do the work. They are more likely to pay while they feel the pressure of the crisis than they are when it has passed.

HOSPITALITY
Welcome but dangerous. Hospitality exposes you to CONCESSION by obligation.

Hospitality is a part of the furniture of social relationships. To refuse hospitality could be unhelpful. To partake, especially at an overly generous level (and your host controls the level), could imply obligations that you did not intend, and raise QUESTIONS from your side about your objectivity under a barrage of hospitality.

Hospitality can be used to:

* weaken your resolve;
* undermine your stamina (late nights, heavy drinking);
* entrap you into indiscretion.

It can also be a genuine expression of a desire to do business together. How do you know which it is? Follow some rules.

❏ Insist on a reciprocity of equivalents: each side is hospitable to the other on the same basis.

❏ Do not compete on the level of hospitality.

❏ Do not socialise late every night (they have a supply of people to keep you at it, while their negotiators rest).

❑ Strictly limit your consumption of food, drink and tobacco.

❑ Schedule your own caucus sessions for most evenings, so that you can refuse an invitation without offence.

❑ Insist that "both sides bear their own costs".

❑ Cut out business lunches (they are mostly unproductive, expensive and disruptive of the afternoon's schedules).

❑ Negotiate in working hours only.

HOSTAGE NEGOTIATION

Hostages are taken either for material gain (cash) or political influence (publicity, revenge, humbling of an enemy, recognition, release of prisoners, change in policies). Terrorist extortion produces a common dilemma: if the demands are conceded, a spate of imitations can be expected; if the demands are not met, the hostages could be harmed.

Governments are less likely to concede demands for political influence than they are demands for material gains.

Terrorists implicitly concede that the government has higher humanitarian standards than their own, irrespective of the rhetoric that justifies their actions, for terrorism is only "successful" if the target is more concerned about the welfare of the victims than is the terrorist. This is a paradox for those terrorising "evil" governments.

The government is constrained by public reaction to its behaviour during a hostage incident.

- If it gives in to save lives, it cannot protect society from terrorist violence.
- If it refuses any deals with the terrorists, resulting in harm to the victims, it fails to protect citizens from the terrorists.
- If it attempts a physical rescue which also harms the victims, it is incompetent.

The government, not the terrorists, is usually put on trial by the media.

H

The INTERESTS of the victims (survival) differ from those of both the terrorists and the government. Behaviour conducive to survival is also their best STRATEGY: a victim has no option. Advice about handling the role of victim includes the following.

- Keep a low profile.
- Show no dissent.
- Do not argue with their beliefs.
- Do not attack them.
- Express no views.
- Show no impatience at all.

If the hostage group is small enough (a dozen or less) there is a possibility of the "Stockholm Syndrome" emerging, that is, a bonding relationship between the terrorists and the victims. This can save lives. But making friends with the terrorists in a larger group is dangerous if the situation turns sour. They need somebody to execute to increase their commitment, and if they shoot their friends clearly they will shoot hostile strangers.

Choosing to negotiate with hostage-takers involves the following objectives.

- The release of the victims unharmed.
- The failure of the terrorists to extract concessions of substance.
- Dissuasion of imitators.

Prevention of terrorism is better than curing it but failing prevention, what are the options?

The terrorists reinforce commitment by threatening to kill hostages. Initially, they set out their demands (which if ludicrously high imply irrational and probably unstable people; if very low they imply media manipulators). They demand to communicate with high officials, they demand publicity, they set deadlines. Either the deadlines are extended or they implement their threats.

The government should leave negotiations to the security forces. It is best that the official in communication with the terrorists is, or is believed to be, of lowly rank. Time is required to find out about the hostage-takers (to choose the most appropriate psychological approach) and to plan intervention by force.

The terrorists do not know for certain which policy the government is pursuing, so they impose short deadlines. They are constrained by the fact that shooting victims reduces the value of their threats (and gives the security forces a publicly acceptable reason for intervening by force).

Tactics include:

- using TIME and isolation in tandem to undermine the terrorists' resolve to continue;
- doing nothing in a hurry, no matter what the THREAT, right from the start;
- doing everything possible to increase the feeling of normality in the immediate vicinity (do not close the airport, its continued functioning helps undermine the terrorists' feeling of self-importance).

Here the media could help (but seldom do). Mentioning the incident on occasional bulletins would help, rather than saturation coverage (not mentioning it at all for a day or so would be best).

Condemning the incident in public undermines the ploy of isolation, while ministers visiting the scene is absolutely counter-productive.

In summary:

☐ Isolate the incident.

☐ Downplay its significance.

☐ Curtail (by self-denial) media coverage.

☐ Engage in negotiations at a low level.

☐ Make no moves in response to acts of violence.

☐ Maintain flexibility of means to achieve firmly set goals.

Remember, winning a hostage crisis is seldom an option (the fact that it occurs is a victory for the terrorists), and your overall OBJECTIVE is to minimise the costs of concluding it without encouraging repetition.

HOTEL

No hotel in the world is always perfect every time. If the incident is serious, consider your remedy: what can they do for you that is proportionate to the incident and within the gift of the management level you are dealing with? Present it without emotional outbursts or threats.

Flouncing out is not a devastating blow to the hotel (unless you have extraordinary BARGAINING leverage). It is more productive to persuade management to agree to your remedy from a positive MOTIVATION to "put things right", than from any fears about losing your custom. People resist giving into COERCION, doubly so when the expected damage of not doing so is minimal.

HOTEL PURCHASE

Valuations of hotels are based on their income-earning capacities. One guide is the annual turnover (GROSS if selling; NET of taxes if buying). Turnover shows the recent trade of the hotel – what it actually does – not what it could do under your management. If there are unusual considerations producing recent turnover, these influence the PRICE.

If buying a hotel from a conglomerate, be wary of inflated turnover figures. Other divisions of the conglomerate could be under instruction to use the hotel services. Once sold to you, these purchases are no longer available.

When buying a hotel from a liquidator be wary of the current trading accounts. The liquidator keeps the hotel open to sell it as a "going concern", and therefore slashes all expenditures to the bone. This reduces cost of sales, and makes the potential profit look better than it is. Repairs and maintenance, even cleaning, can be suspended for a short period.

Base your OFFER price on annual turnover plus stock at valuation (SAV). If you do not want the stock, or any part of it (check all "sell by" dates on booze and supplies), separate it out and require its disposal. Consider changing brewers to avoid paying for unsold previous stocks.

Try for CONTINGENCY PRICING if you doubt the figures.

If there are disposables (valuable furniture, spare land, spare buildings, associated rights) can you sell them to reduce the cost of purchase? (Do not disclose your intentions; the seller could apply your ideas.)

HUSTLE CLOSE
A pressure ploy.

- This plane is leaving right now. It costs 4oz of gold for the last seat, or you learn Arabic.
- You know you'll never get a better deal than this one. If you don't take it right now, I'll ring off and call my lawyers.

Counter: Compare the OFFER against your options. If better, take it; if worse, do not (see BATNA).

IF

A negotiator's most useful two-letter word. All proposals should start with "if" to tell them what they must do for you if you are to do something for them. If they reject your conditions, you are free to amend, postpone, or withdraw your proposal.

"I AM ONLY A SIMPLE GROCER"

A disarming ploy to relax negotiators into indiscretions about their objectives, tactics and hidden intentions. You think you are dealing with a novice because he (or she) claims to be "only a simple grocer", but in reality you are dealing with the owner of the world's largest grocery chain.

"I'M SORRY, I'VE MADE A MISTAKE"

A seller's ploy, close to the ETHICS border. A seller calls you back and apologises because she (or he) has made a mistake in the arithmetic of the order you placed. Instead of the products costing $4.55 each, they are listed in the catalogue at $4.95 each. The mistake was revealed when she placed your order for 1,000 units. She cannot sell them at $4.55 as her boss will not authorise the order. Her explanation is punctured with profuse apologies.

If you believe the seller to be genuine you agree to the higher PRICE. If you do not, you cancel the order. This depends on how important the price mistake was against the total price, and how easy it is to find another seller. Most times buyers succumb, albeit reluctantly, to the ploy.

IMPORTS

Without which we would be poorer (see EXPORTS).

Issues to negotiate with your supplier (the exporting company) include the following.

- ❏ Who bears the foreign exchange RISK?
- ❏ Who bears the cost of credit?
- ❏ Which PRICE prevails: ex-works, cost, insurance and freight (CIF), free on board (FOB)?
- ❏ How is the exporter paid?

INCENTIVE

Motivating by carrot. Offer an incentive for measurable performance and people respond. Supplying incentive gifts (a euphemism for expensive staff presents) is a thriving business.

INDEMNITY

Expensive to buy; risky to do without.

Your professional advice puts you at RISK if somebody fouls up acting upon it. Indemnity insurance protects you against malpractice claims.

The premiums are high because malpractice awards are high; because they are high they are rife; they are rife because claimants are imaginative; claimants are imaginative because lawyers encourage claims to increase the awards; to reduce the awards insurers face high costs; because of the awards and high costs to insurers the premiums are high.

The concept of unlimited liability for professional advisers was meant to concentrate their minds on the advisability of proffering advice.

INFORMATION

Can help or hinder your negotiation.

Information can be valuable when you discover how badly they need your co-operation. Conversely, disclosing your needs can damage your stance.

INHIBITIONS

Concerns that prevent you agreeing to a PROPOSAL. You must decide whether to present your inhibitions openly to the other side and require that they be addressed in their proposals; or leave them unexpressed while presenting proposals that address them. This saves revealing your prejudices.

Listening to what people say reveals their inhibitions.

- They do not TRUST you.
- They are worried about precedent.
- They need to be paid quickly.
- They want to be more selective than the law

allows (sexism, racism, ageism, and so on).
- They are frightened of publicity.
- They do not know if it works.

Your proposals should address their inhibitions.

INTEGRATIVE BARGAINING

Searching for solutions to problems where the negotiators have compatible INTERESTS.

By emphasising the commonality of interests in CONFLICT situations, integrative bargaining can reformulate distributive ZERO SUM disputes into integrative NON-ZERO SUM possibilities.

Integrative bargaining can lead to PROBLEM SOLVING. Considerable TRUST both in you and the process is required (earned not assumed).

A mixture of integrative and DISTRIBUTIVE BARGAINING is more likely to be successful than an approach based totally on one or the other.

INTERESTS

Why you prefer some things to others. Your interests motivate your wants. Interests may be hidden because you are:

- unaware of them;
- embarrassed by them;
- confusing them with your wants.

To uncover interests ask why they want what they are demanding. Is there some other way that you can meet their interests?

When our interests are in conflict with our feelings we face a difficult choice.

INTEREST RATE

The PRICE of money. This varies widely:

- to cover for the opportunity cost of money (how much you can get in an alternative lending activity);
- to cover for the RISK involved;
- to reflect its scarcity value for you (how badly do you want the money?)

INTERPERSONAL ORIENTATION

Psychological insight into how people interact. Negotiators operate along a continuum. They have a high interpersonal orientation if they are responsive to other people. They have a low interpersonal orientation if they prefer to be uninvolved with what is happening to others.

Two negotiators both with high interpersonal orientation:

- engage in co-operative behaviour;
- are likely to solve problems;
- have warm personal relations.

Negotiators with a low interpersonal orientation:

- aim to gain as much as they can without consideration of the others' behaviour;
- do not take anything personally;
- believe that the balance of POWER pushes others to behave competitively or co-operatively (out of confidence or desperation);
- work for their own INTERESTS;
- do not react to the others' behaviour;
- exploit a co-operative stance;
- expect the other negotiators to look after their own interests and to be the best judge of them;
- are not the best team members for a delicate and sensitive negotiation;
- are useful in the early stages of a difficult negotiation (ceasefire, arms control, exchange of prisoners);
- are not useful if relationships need to be warmed;
- offend some negotiators and cause break-downs that have nothing to do with the substantive issues.

Two negotiators with low interpersonal orientations:

- aim to maximise their own interests;
- delay settlement because their moves are based on self-interest only;

- do not generate bonds of TRUST.

INTIMIDATION

Can be overt (bullying, gangsterism) or covert (self-induced).

Covert intimidation is more widespread but hardly noticeable. It works almost entirely through your own mind.

Covert intimidation operates through the power of suggestion. It is the ultimate untested assumption. People covertly intimidate because it works.

INTIMIDATOR

You may never know you have been intimidated covertly.

Well-worn intimidators include the following.

☐ Uncomfortable seating, lower down than the intimidator's.

☐ Poorly positioned seating, such as in a draught, facing the sun or its reflection, or in front of an open door through which other people can hear your conversation.

☐ You are kept waiting.

During the negotiation intimidators may:

☐ take phone calls, speak to secretaries and colleagues and look at their watches;

☐ tell somebody they will be free in a few minutes, when you have just started;

☐ complain about your products or services, and your company;

☐ praise the competition, and appear to know all your rivals by their first names (they keep forgetting yours);

☐ not appear to be paying attention, nor appear interested in anything you say;

☐ not read your literature, not answer QUESTIONS or state their needs, and generally appear to be indifferent.

Intimidators are not rude, they are at work on your perceptions. They aim to force you to move further towards their targets than you intended.

KIDNAP NEGOTIATION

Kidnappers coerce their targets by threatening to harm their victims. Kidnapping poses different problems to that of hostage taking.

- The kidnappers' lair is not known.
- The police are not deployed outside it.
- The kidnappers choose and prepare their location.
- The kidnappers choose when to communicate with the target.
- The police cannot manipulate the environment to isolate the kidnappers.
- The kidnappers do not seek publicity.
- The kidnappers can rest at will.
- The kidnappers choose whether to continue extortion or quit (about 20% of kidnap victims are killed).

The target must decide whether to involve the authorities or to meet the kidnappers' demands. While an individual can be intimidated into ignoring a crime, the state cannot.

Kidnappers are vulnerable during the handover of the ransom because they have to reveal where and when to do so. Laws prohibit the paying of ransom and the entire assets of a target can be frozen to prevent it. These laws can be circumvented if the target has resources outside their jurisdiction and can pay without revealing the details to the authorities.

Targets have to be sure they are dealing with the people who actually hold the victim, because some callers will be bogus (you could use codewords). If interlopers have solved the handover problem, but do not hold the victim, they could get paid by you for nothing. Evidence that the victim is alive, or the property is intact (for example, photographs containing today's newspaper), can be demanded in return for co-operating to pay the ransom, but most evidence is unreliable and, anyway, may be refused.

The authorities are particularly unhappy about those organisations which insure the ransom fee and even arrange to negotiate with the kidnappers and pay it over if required. This form of anti-kidnapping "insurance" goes into effect without incriminating contact between the insurers and the target. Of course, knowledge of a target who has both a vulnerability to a kidnapping and insurance cover is surely a temptation to potential kidnappers.

KILLER LINE

The killer lines that put you on the spot include:

- You'll have to do better than that.
- Give me your best PRICE.

One sentence gets them a major CONCESSION, so they will probably try a few more "killers" to see just how soft you are on price. In fact, you may be bidding downwards against yourself.

Counter: Seek more information.

- What other proposals have they received?
- Is it APPLES AND PEARS?
- If they have a better PRICE, why don't they take it?

Either there is something in your proposal they like, which means it is worth its price, or they are fishing with a price-challenge. Think about your reaction to killer lines.

KILLER QUESTIONS

QUESTIONS to put you on the spot. Answer yes or no and you could be in trouble.

For example: "Is that your final OFFER?" "Yes" ends the negotiation. "No" tells the other negotiators that you have other (better for them) proposals.

Their next question is going to be: "Well, what is your final offer? Is that proposal negotiable?" "Yes" opens the negotiation on your next proposal. "No" ends the negotiation.

Counter: "My proposal is based on the circumstances as I understand them at present, but I am always willing to listen to constructive suggestions that will improve the acceptability of my proposal."

LAST CLEAR CHANCE

A method to apportion blame for an incident. Even if both parties contribute to it, the one with the last clear chance to prevent it is culpable. If you have the last clear chance to avert the incident (STRIKE, failure to supply), you have the unenviable choice of backing off or causing it.

LAW

Best observed, especially when inconvenient.

The rule of law is preferred to the rule of men. For every victim of an unjust law, there are many more victims of unjust conduct. Without the rule of law:

- contracts would be unenforceable;
- property rights would be meaningless;
- promises need not be kept;
- threats would be arbitrary;
- lives would be in jeopardy.

LEASE

An alternative to ownership.

Consider the following points when negotiating a lease AGREEMENT.

❏ Who is the agreement between?

❏ Is there a declaration of non-nominee status? If falsely declared, the property reverts with no compensation and without prejudice to money owed.

❏ Who is guaranteeing the lessee's obligations? If lessee fails to meet obligations, reversion clause applies.

❏ What exactly is being leased?

❏ How much is the rent?

❏ When is it paid (in advance or arrears, monthly, quarterly)?

❏ Is there a premium and on what basis? For the "fixtures and fittings", for the "availability" of the lease?

❏ How long is the lease for?

❏ When does it commence?

❏ Can it be extended and on whose initiative?

❑ When are rent reviews scheduled and are they upward only?

❑ What criteria apply: cost of living, valuation and yield of similar properties?

❑ How are disputes settled?

❑ Is there a "rent-free" period and for how long?

❑ Who pays other charges during this period?

❑ What service charges is the lessee liable for?

❑ Who pays the rates/charges?

❑ Is it a "full repairs and insurance" lease?

❑ What access does the lessor have for inspections?

❑ Who specifies extent of repairs and choice of contractor?

❑ Can lessee sub-let?

❑ With lessor's consent ("not unreasonably withheld")?

❑ Within what duration of the lease (rent-review period only)?

❑ Can lessee assign lease with or without lessor's consent?

❑ On what terms can lessee surrender the lease?

❑ Who pays legal costs of the transaction?

❑ What obligations does tenant have to planning regulations?

❑ If new regulations applied during the tenancy, who pays for them?

❑ What obligations does tenant have to the building's fixtures and fittings and to their good care and upkeep?

❑ What notification must lessee give of intentions to make any alterations to the building?

❑ What regulations must lessee apply? These may include:

- fire certificates;
- prohibitions on storing dangerous or toxic chemicals;
- prohibitions on specified dangerous or illegal (or disreputable?) activities;
- compliance with all laws on occupation and use;
- official cubic space per person employed;

- refraining from causing a nuisance or obstruction of any kind and such like.

❏ Reversion clause to apply for serious or persistent minor breaches at lessor's discretion.

LENDABILITY FACTOR

A subjective judgment (by the lender, not yourself) of the following.

- Your character: are you to be trusted with their money?
- Your record: what your recent past shows.
- Your proposition: what the money is to be used for (how it increases your NET WORTH).
- Your terms: what is in it for the lender?

LETTER OF CREDIT

Facilitates foreign trade; terms are negotiable.

If exporting, require the importer to open a credit with your bank for the value of the goods, CIF or FOB, with the following features.

- Confirmed: importer's bank guarantees payment on production of appropriate shipping documents.
- Irrevocable: prevents importer refusing payment on a pretext.
- Transferable: enables you to endorse it for other transactions.
- Divisible: for part-payments on other deals.

If importing, require the exporter to accept a letter of credit (LOC).

- Make it payable when the goods have passed your inspection (is revocable).
- Trade this for transferability and divisibility, which are direct benefits to the payee.

Practice varies, and reflects the balance of POWER. The wording of a LOC is absolutely crucial, and should be scrutinised carefully. A glance at disputes in case law over LOCs should keep you awake at night.

LEVEL UP THE WORK, LEVEL DOWN THE PRICE

No two bids are the same, except through collusion. Each includes different commitments and features.

Select the commitments and features that you prefer. This is your "levelled-up work specification". Ask the suppliers to re-offer the levelled-up specification at or below the lowest priced quotation. This is your "levelled-down price".

Some suppliers might not re-bid. Others might re-bid and move up on PRICE. If anybody re-bids and meets the levelled-down price, consider awarding them the contract (but beware of BLOCKING BID).

LEVERAGE

BARGAINING power: it is important to know what leverage you have, even if you choose not to apply it.

Almost anything that you have discretion over gives you leverage. Who has leverage?

- Air traffic controllers at holiday time.
- Construction workers when a project is time-critical.
- Exhibition workers when it is due to open.
- Stage hands just before the show.
- Advertisers when TV channels have spare slots.
- TV channels when prime-time slots are full.

Counters: Not easy, otherwise it is not leverage. Raise the stakes.

- Sack the air traffic controllers.
- Cancel the event.
- Lock out strikers for twice as long as they strike.
- Ban advertisers for six months.
- Switch channels, or media.

Lower the stakes.

- Reward negotiators who do not apply leverage unfairly.

- Negotiate other than when leverage can be applied.
- Do not exploit own leverage.
- Reward advertisers who pay full rates with prime-time preference slots.
- Reward TV channels which give preference with off-peak bookings.

LIFEBOAT CLAUSE

When you need a lifeboat, you need a lifeboat. For protection when buying add: . . . *this offer is contingent on the veracity of all statements made by the seller in respect of the proposed sale, including all statements regarding performance, quality, availability and specifications, and approval of the buyer of all matters relevant to the purchase, whether presently known or not, and any other material facts that may affect the buyer's interests.*

You now have an unlimited exit should you find it in your INTERESTS to jump into a lifeboat.

LIFETIME COSTS

Forget them at your peril. Remember the acquisition cost is only part of the PRICE. How much does it cost to maintain the purchased item or service?

LINKING

Opens up BARGAINING possibilities.

Presented with a list of demands, or an OFFER with more than one element, do you deal with each issue separately by treating each one as a distinct mini-negotiation; or link them together on the basis that "nothing is agreed until everything is agreed"?

Separating the issues has an advantage: it narrows down the remaining items in dispute. This blocks off obstructive ploys by parties who hold out for concessions in one area favourable to them for agreement in other areas favourable to others.

Separating the issues has disadvantages, however. The outstanding issues are normally highly contentious (that is why they are outstanding). This leaves very little room for movement by the parties. The settled issues may have been settled "too quickly", curtailing opportunities for additional movement on them. By separating the issues, you could be restricting yourself when you come to deal with the contentious items.

By linking the issues you negotiate where you can get an AGREEMENT, but any agreement is "subject to agreement on all the issues". Linking is much more complex to conduct than single issue BARGAINING. SUMMARISING skills are valuable at any time, but they are at a premium in a linked negotiation.

LIQUIDITY

Highly desirable when you need it, expensive when you do not.

Assets have varying degrees of liquidity. Cash is instant liquidity, but:

- it does not earn interest;
- holding large sums is expensive in forgone earnings;
- it is risky (thieves, fire, flood, carelessness).

Money in a bank with instant access during banking hours is as good as cash. Electronic tellers give 24 hours' liquidity at bank cash dispensers, or by signal to whichever country has its banks open at that moment and in which the payee has an account.

LISTENING

Least successful skill of the below-average negotiator.

It could be the only CONCESSION the other negotiators require: they want somebody to listen to their views, respect them and take account of them, and do not expect more than that.

The message sent is often not the one that is received. People are poor listeners. Even if the message is heard clearly, recall deteriorates rapidly as TIME passes.

Listening to what a negotiator says is hard work. Experiments show how difficult it is to recall accurately even vivid messages, let alone routine ones.

Here are some tips to improve listening.

❒ Ask QUESTIONS for clarification.
❒ Summarise the statements to the satisfaction of the speaker.
❒ Do not interrupt.
❒ Avoid composing your rejection of what they are saying before they finish.
❒ Cease anticipating what they are about to say (you miss the surprises).
❒ Do not judge the message by the messenger.
❒ Treat their statements with respect.
❒ Avoid reacting emotionally to views you find distasteful or otherwise disagreeable.

Here are some tips to help listeners.

❒ Speak clearly and for short periods only.
❒ Summarise your points.
❒ Answer questions briefly.
❒ Avoid diluting your stronger points with weaker points that divert attention from your main message.

LOAN
Against COLLATERAL, a loan can be worthwhile.

It makes sense to borrow other people's money for wealth-creating purposes only (see NET WORTH); it never makes sense to borrow, or to lend, for income.

LOCK-OUT
Supposedly management's answer to a STRIKE: the company refuses work for its employees until certain conditions are met, such as a return to "normal working" or a willingness to undertake specified duties.

Disruptive union tactics can be countered by a lock-out. Unions usually pursue disruptive tactics because:

- they are not sure of the support for an all-out strike;
- they can levy those continuing to work to pay the wages of those sent home without pay for carrying out union instructions;
- they can prolong a dispute for months, causing more problems for the company than for union members.

Should the company impose costs on the employees by sending the entire workforce home? Yes, if this is likely to force a more realistic negotiating stance on the union. No, if the dispute slides into intransigence (see MARTYRDOM).

Alternatively, can the system cope by adapting to the loss of key staff and thus isolate those whose labour has been withdrawn, while imposing levy costs on the rest?

LOSE-LOSE

It happens: neither party can find a COMPROMISE, either because they insist on the other moving only, or because there is no settlement range in their respective positions.

Insisting on winning means they both lose.

M

Major sacrifice gambit

A ploy that manipulates the perceptions of the other negotiator.

Having decided on a traded CONCESSION, you refer to its "significance" and build it up as a major concession as credibly as you can.

If they believe you, they might offer another concession on another issue. Suggest an area where they can compensate you for your "heroic" sacrifice.

Management fees

An alternative to the ownership of capital assets, which are at RISK of expropriation, destruction and deterioration.

Propose a contract to manage assets on their owner's behalf, or to provide a service which the client prefers not to supply itself. Fee income is calculated on "what the market will bear", consistent with a minimum level to cover actual costs.

The benefits include:

- not having large capital projects at risk;
- not having to fund them.

Your net earnings can be equivalent to your earnings from owning and operating the capital commitment.

From the owner's point of view the drawbacks include:

- vulnerability to the managers setting a fee structure which you cannot audit for value;
- where the negotiated fee exceeds the expected profit from the assets, you reduce funds available for depreciation;
- where you reduce the negotiated fee, the professional managers might depart, leaving inefficiently managed assets.

The owner's STRATEGY is to acquire expertise in managing through training local people and to reduce fees towards competitive rates by issuing tenders for the contract.

MANDATE

Defines and limits your authority.

Discretion is a heavy but avoidable responsibility. If you exceed your mandate your deal could be repudiated.

Employees limit the discretion of their representatives by mandating them not to accept any proposal without their approval, and not to accept anything less than the mandated demand. This is often a ploy to enhance commitment rather than an immovable stance.

How can you handle a mandate demand? Not by conceding it, unless you want to receive more mandate demands (see SKINNER'S PIGEON). If you believe it is a COMMITMENT PLOY, do not challenge the commitment; they might demonstrate how strongly they feel committed. If the mandate is the true wish of the employees treat their feelings firmly, though gently, and with a regard to your INTERESTS.

Not all mandate demands survive the first refusal.

MARKET

An unintended human creation which does not discriminate on the basis of sex, religion, status, race, political belief, location, history or intention. No matter who you are, how you feel, how anybody else feels about you or what you do, the market is neutral.

The market:

- processes information about prices;
- can be extensive in a global sense or localised;
- signals discrepancies in wants and the means to meet them, and does so without central or any other kind of direction;
- is robust regarding interference (though not indefinitely);
- is suppressible only in the short term;
- is pervasive across language, cultural and ethnic barriers.

The nature of markets creates the need for

negotiation, for although the market signals a PRICE, that price is the result of infinite adjustments by people to their perceptions of demand and supply. Many of these adjustments are contradictory. People:

- sell when they should hold on;
- buy when they should desist;
- do neither when they should do both.

The constant adjustment of the market, its impermanence for more than a moment and its uncertainty about the future, make negotiating its ideal instrument.

MARTYRDOM
Never underestimate the ability of people to perform acts that are detrimental to their best INTERESTS. Do not assume that people rationally calculate the net benefits of a course of action.

Negotiators can react irrationally, even suicidally, to change. They know that they are going to lose, but their defiance is fed by their emotions.

Martyrdom comforts the defiant, the desperate and the dedicated, which for them far outweighs their sacrifice.

Threatening martyrs plays into their hands. They receive a new lease of life, and public sympathy instead of rejection as a clown.

Martyrs can be exasperating, dangerous and expensive.

MEDIATION
Shares a blurred boundary between ARBITRATION and negotiation.

Negotiators in DEADLOCK might still want to find a settlement, yet neither of them can find a way to move. A mediator seeks a "safe" way for each side to make movement.

Unlike the arbitrator, the mediator does not enforce movement. Unlike the negotiator, the mediator does not trade movement. The mediator first identifies and then informs each negotiator that there is a possibility of movement.

The mediator establishes whether there is a settlement range of which the parties are presently unaware. The mediator is not concerned with the justice of each negotiator's position, how "fair" or "reasonable" it is, or whether it corresponds to the "facts". However, he or she may caution the negotiators that their proposal contains serious obstacles to its acceptance, but it remains the negotiators' responsibility whether to pursue a proposal.

Mediators must:

- take firm charge of the process of dispute settlement;
- be totally indifferent to the settlement;
- not deliberate nor judge the merits of the issues;
- set the rules of the debate;
- not permit interruption of what one person says ("your turn comes later");
- permit any option from the list of possible solutions ("no option is agreed or rejected just because it is discussed");
- insist on no negotiation until all the views of each side have been expressed.

The mediator asks each negotiator to verify to the other the basis of their facts and claims, and to reveal the basis upon which they consider their proposed solutions should be acceptable to the other.

MEMORANDUM OF UNDERSTANDING

Drawn up to commit the parties loosely before the details are agreed. A memorandum of understanding (MOU) outlines the mutual understanding of the negotiators about their intentions to proceed to an AGREEMENT without finally binding them into an irreversible relationship.

Insert a sentence saying "This MOU is subject to final contract" and see that it appears in all correspondence referring to the MOU.

MINIMUM ORDER PLOY

Enhances the value of an order for the seller.

Examples include the following.

- We only sell these in packs of six.
- If we represent you in the purchase of the building, we must also act as letting agents if you acquire it.

Counter: Test their seriousness by your certain choice of the alternative of no order at all.

MINUTES
Minutes record:

- who was present during the negotiation;
- when and where the negotiation took place;
- brief notes on the AGENDA;
- summaries of each negotiator's main views;
- commitments to look at specific topics;
- proposals that are made;
- anything agreed.

Minuting a discussion is not easy even if you are neutral; when you are one of the players it is difficult to do to the complete satisfaction of the other negotiators. Do not succumb to the temptation to "bend" the minute to suit your own INTERESTS. They may fail to notice the alteration, but they are less likely not to notice its consequences. It is interesting that most mistakes in minutes benefit the side which wrote the minutes.

MOTHER HUBBARD
A PRICE pressure ploy implying "the cupboard is bare". The buyer can challenge the seller's price as follows.

- Assert that you desire to buy, but convince them that your budget does not allow you to buy at the price they have quoted. Support this with evidence (for example, minutes of the budget meeting, written instructions).
- Block off all attempts to restructure your budget by running it over two periods, virement across different headings, instalments

and "creative accounting".

- Place the onus of finding a way of reducing the price on the seller.

Close to a sale they will search for ways of coming down to your budget. Some of the changes will be:

- cosmetic but nevertheless valuable to you;
- "creative accounting" (in their accounts not yours);
- tangible to you (shifting the money to after-sales costs);
- a straight cut in price.

How far you place your Mother Hubbard below their quoted price is a matter of judgment: too far and they break off; too close and you pay more than you need to (though any price cut is better than none).

Counter: Difficult if the cupboard really is bare. Try detailed questioning of their budget process, and uncover where the authority lies to change it. It is better to be over their alleged budget because you have priced the "extras" as ADD-ONS than over it with everything priced on an inclusive basis.

MOTIVATION
Other people have baser motives than ourselves. This harmless delusion becomes dangerous when we act as if other negotiators respond only to the motivations we ascribe to them.

Ascribed motive	Competitive action	Co-operative action
Fear	Threaten	Assure
Pride	Mock	Flatter
Hatred	Hate	Love
Loyalty	Exploit	Reward
Money	Minimise	Maximise
Love	Withhold	Requite
Desire	Frustrate	Satisfy
Jealousy	Excite	Calm
Ambition	Block	Assist

To assume that money is the only motivator of all employees ignores a whole range of other motivators, some of which, if recognised and attended to, might be cheaper than an elaborate pay reward system.

MOU
See MEMORANDUM OF UNDERSTANDING.

MUTUALITY PRINCIPLE
The union claims a mutual right with the management to decide on certain issues. Union STRATEGY is to widen the areas of mutuality from conventional wages and working conditions to areas normally reserved as prerogatives of management.

Unions also seek to achieve mutuality on some older areas of managerial prerogatives, such as promotion, selection, hiring, discipline, firing and training.

NASH SOLUTION

Economist's model of the BARGAINING problem.

Nash showed that faced with a choice of achieving some minimum outcome (their "security level") and incrementally improving on that level by accommodating to each other, negotiators maximised the product of their incremental utilities. Nash's solution, by ASSUMPTIONS, abstracts from the skills and bargaining POWER of each individual.

NEED TO GO?

Negotiators who take work with them while travelling, especially abroad, should consider whether they will actually work on their papers on long journeys.

Travel is tiring. Will you open the file late in the evening and set to work? Should papers referring to other negotiations be risked in travel?

NEED TO KNOW

Security in the negotiating team is a prudent precaution. Premature disclosure whether by accident or theft worsens your prospects of a deal.

Negotiating teams should take the following precautions.

❑ Prepare in secure premises.

❑ Adopt a numbering system for all documents and restrict their circulation.

❑ Brief senior personnel in person.

❑ Remember only the negotiators need to see the briefs and the crucial data.

❑ Shred all documents once they have been superseded (and carbons, printer ribbons and disks).

❑ Allow no work to be taken home or on foreign trips.

❑ Enlist positive support for basic security measures from all of the negotiators involved.

❑ Screen the secretariat and the services people (cleaning company employees too).

❑ Relieve colleagues with known personal problems of involvement in a high stress negotiation.

NEEDS THEORY

Meet a negotiator's needs and you are on your way towards agreement, says Gerard Nierenberg, who developed an approach that begins with Maslow's hierarchy of needs (see PSYCHOLOGY OF NEGOTIATION).

Nierenberg categorises six varieties of application to each hierarchy of need, ranked by the degree of control which negotiators may exercise over the outcome. These are as follows.

1 Negotiators working for the opposers' needs: assure, encourage, concede.
2 Negotiators letting the opposers work for their own needs: motivate, permit, challenge.
3 Negotiators working for the opposers' and their own needs: co-operate, COMPROMISE, recognise.
4 Negotiators working against their own needs: waive, relinquish, disavow.
5 Negotiators working against the opposers' needs: veto, embarrass, threaten.
6 Negotiators working against the opposers' and their own needs: thwart, renounce, withdraw.

Each need has an appropriate, or potential, tactic and can be applied to interpersonal, inter-organisational and diplomatic conflicts.

NEGOTIATING LANGUAGE

Some types of language help a negotiator, particularly in the BARGAINING phase. "We require" is more assertive than "we would like" and it is more likely to get attention than a vague expression of desire.

Tell them what you want, and tell them what you are willing to TRADE with them to get it.

Assertive language	Weaker language
I require	I would like
I need	I wish
I must	I hope
I want	I fancy
I insist	I feel

NEGOTIATING SKILL

What distinguishes the above-average negotiator from the rest? Studies of negotiators have identified some of the characteristics of above-average negotiators. If the differences in performance can be replicated with training and practice, below-average negotiators can improve their performance.

Neil Rackham and John Carlisle concluded that the differences in performance were sufficiently consistent as to be identified and run as a training programme. Broadly, above-average negotiators tend to:

- Explore more options.
- Devote much more time to considering areas of potential agreement (though both spend most of their time considering their differences).
- Spend twice as much time considering long-term as opposed to short-term issues (though both spend over 90% of their time on the short-term issues).
- Set objectives within a range rather than a fixed point.
- Leave open the order in which they consider the issues during face-to-face contact.
- Use far fewer irritators (self-praise for their own proposals) which do not persuade and are therefore counter-productive.
- Make far fewer instant counter-proposals.
- Initiate far fewer defend/attack spirals.
- Label their own behaviour before proceeding ("Could I ask a question?"), except when about to disagree, they give their reasons first and then state that they disagree.
- Test their understanding more often.
- Summarise more often.
- Ask many more QUESTIONS.
- Give more information about personal feelings.
- Refrain from diluting arguments with weaker and more vulnerable statements.
- Review the events that had occurred during the negotiation.

NEGOTIATING WITH YOURSELF

A common enough activity. We perceive we are weaker than we really are and we lower our EXPECTATIONS. We anticipate how they are likely to react to our proposals, so we soften them. It is much more fruitful to negotiate with the other party than ourselves; they may be negotiating with themselves instead.

NET

Always smaller than GROSS, so be careful when negotiators refer to net amounts.

The gross amount, less deductibles, equals the net amount. Deductibles are disputable. The share of a net sum, be it profit, income or interest, is of uncertain value to the receiver, and depends on the motives of the calculator. Offer net shares, but demand gross shares.

NET WORTH

Deduct what you owe from what you own: this is your net worth. If it is negative you are vulnerable. You prefer that your net worth is positive and rising.

NO COME-BACKS

The truly one-off deal. No warranties, no promises, no returns, and no responsibility for anything once the deal is concluded. It is *caveat emptor* (and *caveat vendor*). You live with what you bought, or without it, as the case may be.

NO PROBLEM

A reckless CONCESSION.

Q: Can you deliver overnight?
A: No problem.
Q: We need 24-hour call-outs on this equipment.
A: No problem.

"No problem" concessions are wasted. They might be prepared to compensate generously, but you do not know if you do not try.

Put them on the spot.

Q: Are you saying that if we do deliver overnight you will award us the contract?

Q: If we can offer a 24-hour service, do we get the business?

NO SALE, NO FEE

A version of CONTINGENCY PRICING. Payment for services is based exclusively on results.

"No fee" could still involve costs (advertising and other expenses) even when no sale occurred. If a sale takes place, but the fee-earner was not responsible for the sale, does he or she still get a fee?

People offering "no sale, no fee" contracts are often looking to build a client list, or are desperate for work, or are speculative agents.

NOAH'S ARK

A buyer's pressure ploy: "You'll have to do better than that because your rivals are quoting better prices than you are." It is almost always a bluff. It has been part of the buyer's repertoire of winning moves for so long that Noah let two of them on board.

Sometimes buyers do have a better PRICE but more often they do not have comparable packages from the sellers (see APPLES AND PEARS).

- Comparable packages but different prices. If you drop your price the buyer is better off by the difference and can induce your rivals to follow suit against you (see DUTCH AUCTION).
- Non-comparable packages and therefore non-comparable prices. If you believe that the proposals are comparable and you reduce your price, the buyer is better off.
- Rivals' prices are higher (or you believe them to be). If you reduce your prices to defeat rivals (real or imagined) the buyer is better off.

Because the Noah's Ark is beneficial to buyers it is the most persistent ploy in negotiations all over the world, used by generation after generation.

Counter:

- Question the buyer's comparisons.
- Refuse to react unless you can compare the quotes direct.
- Ask why the buyer is dealing with you if your rivals' quotes are better.

NON-VERBAL BEHAVIOUR

55% of a negotiator's message is perceived non-verbally; only 7% depends on what is said, and 38% on how it is said.

It is not that a single gesture reveals all but how gestures fit in with what we are trying to say. If they contradict our words, then the message received is different from the one sent.

- Crowding the private space of the other negotiator or pumping a stranger's hand-shake as if with a long-lost friend can destroy the intended effect.
- Touching the face, rubbing the cheek, covering the mouth and such like can mean someone is being less than candid; it can also mean that they have an itch or they were eating garlic last night.
- Chin stroking can mean they are coming to a decision. It is not sensible to interrupt their thoughts at this point.
- If the other negotiator sits back, folds his or her arms and is about to say something, it is almost certainly going to be "no", so swift intervention to go over the positive points in your proposal might be helpful.
- Hands folded across the chest are defensive, suggesting that the other negotiator does not accept what you have said.

Bashing the same point only forces the person to dig in. Perhaps some QUESTIONS would reveal what is wrong, from the listener's point of view, with your message?

Non-verbal behaviour is underrated by some people and overrated by others. A brilliantly manipulated message is unlikely to be successful if the content is unacceptable, and a badly sent message, that would otherwise be acceptable, could be rejected because the listener has grave doubts about your true intentions.

NON-ZERO SUM

What you gain is not at my expense (see ZERO SUM). The sum of the positive gains is greater than zero.

Suppose you are negotiating several issues, such as:

- PRICE per unit;
- quantity to be delivered;
- when payment is to be made;
- specification;
- policy on returns of defective units.

Your INTERESTS as the buyer may be best served by a delayed payment to suit your cash flow, a large quantity in stock to cover surges in demand and a flexible returns policy to cover for breakages. The seller may be interested in a premium price to move the product "upmarket", large production runs to reduce unit costs and a specification that reduces inspection costs.

Trading a higher unit price for delayed payment, a different specification for a flexible returns policy and matching each other's needs for large production and order quantities, provides each of you with a non-zero sum settlement. You both make gains without diminishing the other's gains.

NOT NEGOTIABLE

A pressure ploy. Stake out a non-negotiable area, refuse to budge, and force the other negotiator to accept your exclusion of issues from negotiation.

The problem comes if what you are excluding from the negotiation is the central issue that the other negotiator wishes to negotiate about.

Some issues are non-negotiable, and we prefer to resolve the dispute by other means (war, litigation). But excluding issues does not make them non-negotiable, otherwise negotiators would narrow the negotiable issues to the ones they felt strongest in, or the ones they were least concerned about.

NOTHING IS AGREED

Nothing is agreed until everything is agreed.

Listening to a proposition does not commit you to agreeing to it (do not interrupt). Asking QUES-TIONS about a proposition does not signify you agree with it.

Assert regularly that agreement on one issue is not final and must await consideration of the whole package (see LINKING).

OBJECTION

A defensive move, signalling INHIBITIONS about your proposal. Unanswered, objections fuel the inhibitions of the objector.

Do not interrupt well-worn objections with well-worn answers.

☐ Listen to the objection.

☐ Ask QUESTIONS for clarification.

☐ Show empathy ("Yes, I see what you are getting at."), not contempt ("Yes, it's true that some less informed people do worry about that.")

☐ Address the objection with a full and frank exposition to eliminate their concerns.

☐ If their worries are founded on a misconception, gently correct it, and support with a review of the benefits. Ask positively if their anxieties have been satisfied.

☐ When the objection refers to something your service does not cover avoid trying to bluff your way round it.

☐ Direct their attention to how what they are worried about compares with the benefits from the rest of your proposal.

An objection answered is a step towards agreement.

OBJECTIVE

Quantified objectives are meaningful; non-quantifiable objectives are suspect.

If your objectives are vague – "a better deal", "happier employees" – quantify them by considering the steps needed to achieve them.

• What constitutes a better deal?
• What would make the employees happier?

Set a range rather than choose a fixed number. A range gives you negotiating flexibility and forces you to consider alternative trade-offs (your nascent negotiating STRATEGY).

The more thoroughly you prepare your

objectives, across the maximum number of TRADABLES, the more confident you will be in negotiation.

OFF THE RECORD

One way out of DEADLOCK is through an off-the-record discussion. The principals can meet for a private discussion, out of earshot of their colleagues, and agree to settle. If using a "washroom" ADJOURNMENT, check the stalls first in case an unnoticed outraged colleague puts the private talks on the record.

Use off-the-record moves only with negotiators you know well and TRUST.

OFF-SET

Increasingly common and a restriction on free trade. No direct transfer takes place between the supply of goods and the off-set activity.

Off-sets are largely political counters to lobbying against foreign suppliers.

An off-set deal is meant to bring new work to the domestic economy, but it is often merely work that would be placed in the country anyway.

OFFER

Can be tentative or specific but should always be conditional: if you do such and such, then I will do so and so.

When making tentative offers be specific about what they must do for you and be vague about what you could do in return.

Being too specific reveals your hand, causing them to revise their EXPECTATIONS to your disadvantage. The non-specific offer is suitable for the ADD-ON.

BARGAINING offers are always:

- conditional;
- specific.

If they say "yes" to a specific offer you have an AGREEMENT.

OFFER THEY MUST REFUSE

An OFFER deliberately set to be rejected. Contractors overloaded with work BID high to avoid winning a contract when not bidding at all would antagonise the buyer and endanger future opportunities.

To be used when you wish to avoid:

- low profit contracts;
- contracts below a minimum value;
- places where you do not want to go;
- people you prefer not to deal with.

Introduce unacceptable conditions, or demands that are outside the other negotiator's limits, or by deliberately declaring something to be NOT NEGOTIABLE that is vital to them.

Problem: Sometimes the "offer they must refuse" is accepted and you are left to get on with it.

ON TAKING IT PERSONALLY

Negotiators are human: they get upset. Occasionally even seasoned negotiators get extremely angry, make threats, raise their voices, shout, curse and remonstrate. Sometimes they walk out and protest at the other negotiator's behaviour.

Most negotiators slip into unprofessional involvement some of the time. In negotiating, do not take it personally or we will all be worse off.

ONE-OFFER-ONLY

Procedure whereby suppliers get one chance to offer their best PRICE in competition with others.

It is best used for the regular purchase of standard products that are well specified. It can also be used occasionally for expensive mandatory services (audits, banking and legal services, pension fund management, insurance, and so on). Test the market by calling for tenders for your business for fixed periods of, say, 2–3 years.

If the specification is unambiguous, there is nothing but price to negotiate. If there is no collusion between sellers, you can be sure of a competitive price (somebody is almost always willing to DISCOUNT a price for business).

If the specification is complex, or the purchase is so separated in time as to be unusual, purchase by negotiation. Not being too sure about what you want could lead you to specify something that a negotiation could improve upon.

ONE PRICE, ONE PACKAGE

A seller's defensive ploy. You can expect the other negotiators to push you either on the PRICE or on the package, or both. To clinch the deal they "need" this or that extra, or demand them as add-ons inclusive of your quoted price (see YES, BUT).

❏ Apply the principle "this package, this price; that package, that price".

❏ Flush out all the extras or changes that the buyer wants to your proposed package. This blocks off a "yes, but" approach.

❏ Price these as another package.

❏ TRADE off changes in the package against the change in the price.

Failing to price package changes undermines their value (free gifts are seldom appreciated), and you miss an opportunity to educate the buyer that you negotiate by trading not by unilaterally conceding.

Precedents are promises for the future.

ONE-TRUCK CONTRACTS

A risky way to do business. You undertake a transaction with a minimum of discussion about the contingencies that might arise. If these contingencies are expensive, there is a RISK of a liability claim.

Hiring a truck with a minimum of fuss has its advantages: "one truck, $150 a day rental". But trucks are used for some purpose, and in using a truck all kinds of possibilities emerge.

- Who pays for repairs while on hire?
- Who recovers the vehicle if it breaks down?
- Who pays for fuel?
- Is it replaced if it is stolen or breaks down?
- Who is legally liable for its mechanical condition?
- Is it warranted for the use to which it is to be put?

Profitable rental companies have pre-printed contracts with every imaginable contingency covered either in detail or through LIFEBOAT CLAUSES (which is why they are profitable). Consider the possible contingencies in your deals and negotiate for them to be covered.

OPTION

Protection against gazumping. When buying, offer the seller an option instead of a deposit. This "locks in" the seller to the transaction and protects you from gazumping.

Offer a cash consideration for the purchase of a legally binding option to buy the property by a given date for an agreed PRICE. Court awards against defaulting sellers deter gazumpers. If for any reason you fail to buy the property, the seller keeps your option money. When you exercise your option to buy, set the option money against the purchase price.

Will a seller accept an option to purchase AGREEMENT? That depends on the terms of the option.

Sellers have an interest in raising the price of the option; the higher it is the more determined the buyer will be to exercise the option. If the option price is acceptable to you, it does not matter if the buyer sells on the same property at a higher price. It is like having estate agents pay you for selling your property, which is better than paying them anything from 1% to 3%.

OR ELSE

An ultimatum ploy: "Either you meet our demands, or else we call a strike."

Such ploys can provoke the very resistance they are trying to overcome. If they believe that your THREAT is empty, or can be ridden out, they might choose to take the "or else" consequences rather than give in. They might be defiant enough to take the "or else" option, even though you have overwhelming POWER.

ORDER-TAKING

A sign of a jaded sales force. Sellers who merely meet customers to take their regular orders are missing opportunities to negotiate better orders. It might be cheaper for a company selling from a regular low-value list to use a telephone-sales operation.

OVER-AND-UNDER PLOY

The impossible response to the impossible demand. The other negotiator sometimes springs an impossible demand upon you: "Give me 5% for a three-day settlement discount."

Spring back an over-and-under: "If you agree to a 5% premium for late payment."

PACKAGING

Unwrapping and rewrapping proposals to make them mutually acceptable. By repackaging the mutually contradictory or overlapping parts of competing proposals you move towards BARGAINING.

Packages address the INTERESTS and INHIBITIONS of each party. If they are keen on the money (interest) but are worried about getting paid (inhibition), repackage your proposal to meet these requirements without jeopardising your own.

- Can you repackage them in a different way?
- What are the shared interests in particular options?
- Can you TRADE movement on one option for movement on a less important option?
- What might you want for offering them what they want?

PADDING

A negotiating margin. The padded PRICE gives sellers negotiating room. When the buyer expects some movement and you have no room to move, you could end up losing the business, or buying it at the expense of your profits.

Pad prices when:

- you anticipate last-minute demands;
- they do not have final AUTHORITY;
- you expect a competitive re-bid ploy;
- dealing with PRICE blind clients;
- you can avoid a COST BREAKDOWN;
- you have to wait for your money;
- a COUNTER-TRADE proposition is likely;
- whenever you can get away with it.

PARTNER

A partner shares your problems and the profits. Disputes between partners originate from differing perceptions of how each fits into the future direction of the business. Partnerships that break up are more complicated than a divorce so it is better to negotiate terms before the partnership is formed rather than when a break-up is imminent:

- on how the assets and liabilities will be shared in the event of a dissolution or divorce;
- on the rules for removing somebody from the partnership who is incompetent or otherwise no longer suitable.

You feel the need for a partner most when you need access to capital or contacts. But why give away things you will value later for things you value now, if the consequence is that you have to share everything (the worth of the business, plus its profits) long after your initial needs have been met. Can you offer a high return on the capital invested rather than a partnership? Once you pay the lender off, everything you created remains yours.

PATENTS AND LICENCES

Products and services can be licensed. The licensor receives income for creating a product or service which the licensee exploits in a defined territory.

Consider the following when negotiating licences.

❏ What is the licensor granting to the licensee and for which territory?

❏ What is the licensee entitled to market or sell?

❏ Which specific patents, trademarks and know-how is the licensor licensing?

❏ How exclusive is the licence?

❏ Is the licensee allowed to sell outside the territory?

❏ Can the licensor also supply, independently of the licensee, into the licensee's territory?

❏ Are other licensees of the licensor permitted to sell or supply in the licensee's territory?

❏ If the licensee fails to meet market targets, or to supply known demands for the licensor's products or services, can the licensor supply direct, or contract with another licensee to do the same?

❏ How much does the licensee pay for the licence and when?

☐ Is the licence fee a royalty on GROSS or NET turnover?

☐ If net, how is this defined?

☐ How regular are the payments to be?

☐ What separate accounts should the licensee keep? How regularly may they be inspected? Who shall audit them?

☐ How long should the AGREEMENT last?

☐ What notice is required to terminate the agreement?

☐ Under what conditions can premature termination occur (breach of contract, FORCE MAJEURE, bankruptcy of licensee, merger or takeover by another company)?

☐ What must the licensee undertake when the licence is revoked for any reason? What restrictions on the licensee are imposed? What happens to all current stocks or client services?

☐ What obligations are there on the licensee to preserve confidentiality both in and out of contract?

☐ What guarantee of quality must the licensee give in respect of the production or supply of the licensor's goods or services?

☐ What restrictions are to be imposed on the licensee for supplying similar goods or services?

☐ What training and support is the licensor to supply to the licensee, and who meets the costs?

☐ How are disputes between the licensor and the licensee to be resolved and which country's law applies?

PATIENCE

More than a virtue, patience is imperative. TIME is the most expensive cost of negotiating. Patience reduces time pressures.

- If the negotiation is likely to be a long one arrange coverage of senior staff so that other work does not suffer.
- Rotate staff to reduce isolation and fatigue.
- Reduce your reliance on the outcome of the negotiation by competing for other work.
- If you desperately need the business from a long-haul negotiation, consider your BATNA.
- Sit it out, but send patient people to negotiate.

- Whoever has the least patience concedes faster.

PENALTY CLAUSE
Assurance against failure to comply with promises. The penalty can be a fixed or escalating sum.

When pressing for penalty clauses assert that if they have confidence in their performance they have nothing to fear from them.

Resist penalties if the nature of the work creates unique uncertainties, such as:

- unforeseeable geological conditions;
- narrow weather windows;
- special safety hazards;
- political instabilities that threaten access and egress;
- difficult legal complications;
- dependence on suppliers outside your control;
- technological frontiers;
- untested designs;
- reliance on client's data;
- subjection to client's changeable specifications and managerial directions.

Your performance guarantees only operate if:

- spares, inputs and materials meet your own specifications;
- everybody connected with the process is trained to your standards;
- the working environment is suitable for the process;
- you have the right to on-site inspection, to replace or repair, and to decide if any working practice is in violation of your warranties.

Insist that the penalty clock stops if delays are caused by the client's failure to meet obligations; it is re-started (at your confirmation) only when the client complies; this moves all consequential critical dates to new later dates, and not just the dates of the immediately affected segment.

Penalty clauses are sometimes used to beat "unfair trading", dumping or illegal subsidy rules. The supplier quotes a PRICE with a substantial delivery penalty and ensures delivery is delayed. The penalties come into force and reduce the price. You get a reputation for poor delivery, but you get the business.

PENDULUM ARBITRATION

The arbitrator must choose one or other negotiator's FINAL OFFER and not seek a COMPROMISE between them.

A negotiator could be encouraged to refuse to settle because an arbitrator's decision is a compromise between the two final offers and improvement in the other negotiator's "final offer" is bound to result.

When, however, the arbitrator is using pendulum arbitration the negotiator must ensure that the final offer is not too extreme because the arbitrator is likely to choose the other negotiator's less extreme position. Adjusting the final pre-pendulum arbitration offer to make it attractive to the arbitrator also makes it more attractive to the other negotiator. When both negotiators do this they become more conciliatory, which improves their chances of finding a solution.

PERCEPTION

Seeing ourselves as nobody else does.

Other people's behaviour influences your perceptions and what you perceive confirms, or amends, your ASPIRATIONS. The other negotiators attempt to influence your perceptions in order to:

- restructure them in their favour;
- shake your faith in the viability of your current offer;
- increase the sense of inevitability of settling at their current offer.

You structure your opponent's perceptions by your apparent:

- willingness to DEADLOCK;
- indifference to settling quickly;
- confidence that you have options;
- resolve not to COMPROMISE;
- professional success;
- confidence in your current proposal;
- willingness to listen;
- reasonableness.

Use the following ploys.

- Weaken your opponents' confidence. Ask for the criteria, method of calculation, statement of the "facts", and references to precedent or convention which support their case; then look for inconsistencies, alternative "facts", dubious ASSUMPTIONS, omissions and unwarranted conclusions.
- Deter resort to COERCION. Assert your desire for a negotiated settlement to save avoidable costs to both sides. Adjourn to "cool off" and think through the consequences of not coming to an AGREEMENT. Show willingness to continue negotiations for "as long as it takes".
- Enhance the viability of your own proposals. Show confidence in your presentation, your grasp of detail, your willingness to understand their needs and to consider options that bridge your differences, and your intention of coming to an agreement as soon as possible (although you are more than willing to wait, if needs be).

PERFORMANCE BOND

Varying degrees of onerous burdens imposed by powerful buyers on desperate sellers. Originally the performance bond protected the client from shoddy work.

A performance bond concentrates your efforts to deliver your promises. If you fail, the buyer cashes the bond and receives compensation.

The performance bond could be irrevocable and unconditional and the buyer may have a right to cash it, as the fancy takes him or her. To agree to this is an act of reckless desperation, irrespective of the quality of your performance. Refusal to agree to a performance bond disqualifies you on the grounds that you have something to fear, so you agree.

Performance bonds shift the RISK from the buyer to the seller (if buying, demand one). The risk is transformed from one of your performance into one of whether the buyer will invoke payment regardless of your performance. The POWER balance determines whether you agree to their terms.

Unscrupulous officials sometimes press for a bribe as an inducement for them not to present the bond for payment.

PERRY MASON PLOY

Behaving like legal counsel and interrogating the party you are trying to negotiate an AGREEMENT with.

The ploy consists of asking a string of QUESTIONS, the answers to which are at first apparently innocuous. As they receive the answer "yes", they move in for the "guilty" question.

The ploy is illegitimate. There is no connection between the lead-in questions and the ultimate question. If you answer their questions they pronounce you "guilty". Hence, best not to answer any questions at all.

Counter: Ask "What exactly are you getting at?"

PERSONAL RELATIONSHIPS

Never underestimate their value. Only trespass on them once. Do not rely on them. Business is business.

While you seek to cultivate sound personal relationships based on demonstrated TRUST and reliability, you must recognise that other people's commitment to your INTERESTS, when the bullet slides into the breach, is fragile.

Commercial negotiators, diplomats and bargaining agents inevitably form relationships, if only from getting to know each other. These relationships are important, however tentative they may be, for negotiating with somebody you do not know is more difficult than negotiating with somebody you do.

The basic principle of establishing a personal negotiating relationship is to assist them to achieve their OBJECTIVE within the boundaries of your own. In short: do not take undue advantage of their predicament.

PERSUASION

The most common form of discourse when you face a problem.

People whose INTERESTS are different from yours are not easily persuaded if the stakes are important to them. When they are not persuaded by your reasonable, logical and sensible statements, you are frustrated, you become annoyed, you perceive a wickedness in their inability to see your point of view. The result is an ARGUMENT.

You limit the likelihood of failure by:

- Attempting to persuade them of simple, easy to agree points, rather than complex, controversial issues.
- Emphasising your eagerness for reaching an AGREEMENT, not for forcing them to comply (that is, do not mix persuasion with threats).
- Restricting yourself to a few robust arguments in favour of your position that stand up to scrutiny rather than diluting them with spurious arguments that collapse as soon as the weakest is challenged.
- Appealing to their self-interest rather than recognition of what you deserve.

POSITIONAL BARGAINING

Build yourself a position and fortify it. Negotiators can get stuck into defending positions instead of seeking a solution. Defending a position can lead to attacking the other party's position, which leads to destructive ARGUMENT and DEADLOCK.

Repetitive defences of positions harden the

negotiators' stances and stifle creativity (see PRINCIPLES 2).

POWER

Like the wind, felt rather than seen. You have power over the other negotiators to the extent that you can induce them to do something they would otherwise not do; and vice versa.

Your BARGAINING power, as is the other negotiator's, is a function of the relative costs of disagreement to each of you. Specifically:

$$\text{your bargaining power} = \frac{\text{cost to them of rejecting your terms}}{\text{cost to them of accepting your terms}}$$

$$\text{their bargaining power} = \frac{\text{cost to you of rejecting their terms}}{\text{cost to you of accepting their terms}}$$

In general, if your power ratio is greater than unity (the costs of rejection are larger than the costs of acceptance), then you have bargaining power over the other side.

Operational content can be derived by calculating the actual costs of rejecting their OFFER. These costs must be probabilistic: there is no certainty that their last offer is their FINAL OFFER, nor that the threatened, or implied, consequence (STRIKE, LOCK-OUT, cancelled contract, divorce, war, and so on) will materialise. Moreover, your estimates of the costs of accepting their last offer may be pessimistic.

Power is subjective. You perceive their power according to many influences on your mind, some of them unconscious, some of them mistaken and some manipulated by them.

PRAISING THE PRODUCT

Do not. It only encourages them to charge more for supplying it.

PRE-EMPTIVE BID

An attempt to jump a queue before an AUCTION. You bid an amount sufficient to induce the owner to accept it in preference to waiting for the auction. If the BID is "high" enough, the inducement is plain.

To apply extra pressure:

- make your pre-emptive bid conditional on its almost immediate acceptance;
- state that if the bid is rejected you will not re-bid subsequently at any PRICE whatsoever. Mean it.

PREMIUM PRICING

Premium products are marketed at higher prices than others. The price mark-up may not reflect anything substantial in terms of product differences. If the other negotiators perceive your product to be superior to substitutes, they might be persuaded to pay a premium price.

PREPARATION

Jewel in the crown of effective negotiation. Get this right and your performance in the negotiation dramatically improves.

The best preparation is knowing your business better than anybody else. If you do not know your business well enough, you can rely on your rivals to teach you.

❑ What are my INTERESTS?

❑ What are the issues? Itemise the details for negotiation.

❑ What do I want for each issue?

❑ How important is each want to me? Prioritise them using:

- high importance (must get or definitely no deal);
- medium importance (intend to get or perhaps no deal);
- low importance (like to get but will still deal).

❑ What are my entry offers? Quantify them.

❑ What are my exit offers?

❑ What do I not want, and how badly? (See INHIBITIONS.)

❑ What might the other negotiators want?

❑ What might be their entry offers?

❑ How might they prioritise their wants?

❑ What information have I got that helps me?

❑ What information could hinder me if disclosed?

❑ What information do I need to verify my ASSUMPTIONS?

❑ What is my STRATEGY? Keep it simple.

❑ What happens if it is not working? Select a fall-back strategy.

Write everything down. A preparation planner is a useful tool for developing your ideas (see Figure 2). Your wants are listed in a column down the left hand side of the paper.

- Allocate degrees of importance to your wants (high, medium, low) and collect them together in the column.
- Establish a range rather than a fixed number for each want.
- Write your entry offer for each want on the left and your exit offer on the right.

Figure 2 **Preparation planner objectives**

Wants	Importance	Entry offer	Exit offer
	High		
	Medium		
	Low		

Price

First unassailable law of the MARKET: the selling price of something is not what it cost its owner, but what it is worth to the keenest person to acquire it.

The total revenue from sales equals price per item times quantity sold. The total cost from producing the items equals cost per item times quantity produced. If total revenue minus total cost is greater than zero you make a profit. If it is not, you do not. To stay in business, find enough buyers keen to acquire your output at a price which raises total revenue above total costs.

The trouble is that your costs are your affair but your selling price is set by the market.

All companies' problems boil down to price. To survive profitably you must drive down costs per unit (search for efficiency) and find the price that captures the most profitable total revenue (net of marketing costs).

Troubles begin when companies kid themselves by versions of:

- altering attributions across cost headings;
- changing depreciation practice, and so on;
- "marginal cost pricing";
- pricing for "contribution to overheads";
- pricing to "fill unused capacity";
- pricing to "clear the unsaleable stock".

Price negotiation

Prices are determined by the MARKET, but you do not sell to markets, you sell to people, and these people do not have perfect information. Imperfect information is both your edge and your torment.

If buyers are queueing six deep to buy your stock, your PRICE will be higher than if you are in a six-deep queue of sellers waiting to sell it. But if it is "down to price" alone, consider getting out of that line of business.

A price negotiation is a ZERO SUM game. Your most profitable strategies include the following.

- ☐ Widen the negotiation from price to other TRADABLES.
- ☐ Separate yourself from the competition.
- ☐ Form a queue with only one person in it: yourself.
- ☐ Go for the big numbers (test the quantity discounts available from sellers; test the total revenue available from buyers).
- ☐ Go for the ADD-ONS.
- ☐ Test the buyer's price sensitivity.
- ☐ Test the seller's mark-up.
- ☐ Go for the co-operative relationship.
- ☐ Test the buyer's INTERESTS.
- ☐ Test the seller's reliability.
- ☐ Go for the mutual WIN-WIN.
- ☐ Test the buyer's room for manoeuvre.
- ☐ Test the seller's room for manoeuvre.
- ☐ Enter not too close to your exit price.

PRICE VERSUS COST

A ploy to protect a PRICE from a buyer's challenge. For example:

Seller: Do you want low price or low cost?
Buyer: I don't follow you.
Seller: Low-priced products cost more when you use them. They break down more often and have a short life.
Buyer: You just want me to pay your high price?
Seller: Sure I want you to pay my price, but I also want you to benefit from a longer-lasting product with lower costs over its longer life than a cheapie.
Buyer: So?
Seller: Well, you pay my price only once, but how many times will you pay for the cheapie?

PRICE WAR

Avoid it. Move into some other business. Move upmarket or move downmarket or move sideways, but do not join in.

Price wars are won by the big battalions. If your market share is 1%, you will not drive a *Fortune 500* competitor out of the market by slashing your prices. The competitor could give your 1% volume free to your customers and wait until you ran out of breath.

If you cannot keep out of a price war the objective is to survive, not to win (for there are no winners).

PRINCIPAL

The organ grinder. The advantages of dealing with principals are as follows.

- They make the final decision.
- They can authorise changes.
- They can accept unusual offers.
- They are closest to the money.
- They can come to a decision quickly.
- You have equal status.
- You eliminate wallies.

The disadvantages of dealing with principals are as follows.

- There is no appeal against their final decision.
- They are not always on top of the detail.
- They are too busy for slow-moving negotiations.
- They do not believe in equal status.
- They are emotionally involved with their properties.
- Some of them are wallies.

PRINCIPLES 1

Sometimes it is necessary to rise above them.

Negotiators who affirm to having principles often mean the beliefs that sanctify their prejudices. These people are extremely difficult to negotiate with, for their "principles" are a barrier to movement.

PRINCIPLES 2

"Never yield to pressure, only to principle." (Roger Fisher and Bill Ury)

General principles that are independent of the

negotiators are seen as aids to agreement. Instead of battling over conflicting demands, the negotiators search for objective criteria to judge the merits of alternative solutions.

If objective criteria are agreed (and this is not certain: see FORMULA BARGAINING), these become the principles that determine the joint solution.

You appeal to criteria independent of both of you.

- "Fair standards" or "fairness" generally.
- Market valuation.
- Scientific measurement.
- Legal precedent.
- Actual costs.
- Agreed objectives.
- Equalisation of misery/profits/risks.

This does not avoid a dispute about the criteria. You may have to modify your demands in the light of the mutually chosen criteria and you must be willing to do so.

If pressure is applied insist on determining the issue by principles. If they have the POWER, however, it is usually decided their way, not yours. This is the weakness of this principled approach: there is seldom a unique set of objective criteria for each dispute. Indeed, the parties can DEADLOCK over the choice of criteria, with each backing a selection that enhances its own position, taking us back to the problems of POSITIONAL BARGAINING.

PRIORITIES

Best sorted out in PREPARATION, not while negotiating face-to-face.

Wants are not all weighted with the same degree of priority, otherwise there would be little room for movement. Some issues are more important than others and their ranking should be decided beforehand.

It is in the difference in priorities with which the negotiators approach the issues that the solution is found.

- Anything that the other negotiators value more than you is open to a TRADE for those things that you value more than them.
- It is not what it is worth to you which is decisive; it is the relative value to them.
- Your low priorities are not "giveaways"; they may value them more than you do.
- Paradoxically, the more they value particular outcomes the more POWER they give you if you value them less than they do.
- Power is balanced when the values of the issues are inversely related.

Events in the negotiation revise your priorities. Establishing your priorities is an organising not a stultifying activity. It ensures a grasp of the detail.

PRISONER'S DILEMMA

There is no correct solution to a dilemma; that is why it is a dilemma.

You face many dilemmas in negotiating: where to open, when to move, whether to agree or DEADLOCK. You resolve the dilemma by whatever choice you make but your choice cannot be reversed.

Prisoner's dilemma is a mind game that illustrates the meaning of a dilemma. Two suspects are questioned by the District Attorney (DA) who suspects them of having committed a major crime, but does not have enough evidence to convict them. The DA does have enough evidence to convict them both of a lesser offence.

The prisoners are interviewed in separate rooms with no possibility of communication. They are each given a choice between confessing and not confessing to the serious crime. The DA's proposition is as follows.

- If you confess, but your partner does not, you turn state's evidence and go free, and your partner gets 20 years.
- If you both confess you each get ten years.
- If neither confesses, you get five years each for the lesser offence.

If you were a prisoner, what would you do? Your consideration of the options and your hesitation between them is an example of a dilemma.

Dilemmas are relevant to the negotiating situation. They help spell out the implications of the COMPETITIVE STYLE and the CO-OPERATIVE STYLE of behaviour. Going for short-term gains can severely damage your long-term gains. Going for long-term gains (not exploiting your BARGAINING position) could be beneficial in the long run, but it is also risky in the short run if you are modifying your gains with someone who regards you as a one-off temporary partner. (See TIT-FOR-TAT.)

PROBLEM-SOLVING

Requires TRUST between the parties and confidence in each other's motives. Unilateral attempts to problem-solve a dispute expose you to STRATEGIC INTERACTION by the other negotiators if they continue to use a COMPETITIVE STYLE.

Problem-solvers aim to:

- maximise joint gains;
- focus on common INTERESTS, not differences;
- be non-confrontational and non-judgmental;
- apply standards of "fairness", "common sense" and "reasonableness" (see PRINCIPLES 2).

They believe the other negotiators can be motivated to replace egoism with enlightened self-interest.

PROCEDURE

Formal negotiating procedures are common in COLLECTIVE BARGAINING.

Procedure agreements between a TRADE UNION and an employer set out formal recognition of each side's rights and INTERESTS.

Employees are required to take up any GRIEVANCE they have with their immediate manager in the first instance. A FAILURE TO AGREE means the next level of management must be contacted, usually through, or accompanied by, an officially recognised shop steward.

If the shop stewards cannot settle the grievance, the local union official will be accorded higher-level access with the company. Where the company has more than one plant, the higher-level management will deal with the national officials of the union.

A grievance that survives the early opportunities for resolving it is usually of significance to both sides. The union will take a view on the significance of the member's grievance and how it relates to union policy. In theory this filters out trivial grievances. In practice the union removes the filter when it wishes to impose pressure on the company by letting grievances through to use up management time.

Companies negotiating formal procedures with a union should do the following.

❏ Reject "closed shops" or "100% union membership agreements".

❏ Require that membership remain a voluntary decision of the employees.

❏ Insist that non-members will not be discriminated against in any respect (they will have a parallel grievance procedure).

❏ Require the AGREEMENT to be of fixed, rather than indefinite, duration.

❏ Include a statement that "no accredited shop steward will be accorded special privileges as an employee and at all times will be subject to the normal disciplinary rules that apply to all employees".

❏ Reserve their right to communicate directly with all employees on any matters, and at no time concede this as an exclusive right of the union.

❏ Exercise this right on a regular basis, as communicating with employees only in crises with the union can be counter-productive.

PROGRESS PAYMENT

Reduces exposure on long lead-time projects. Paying for materials for major construction projects imposes costs on the supplier (the capital tied up has a cost in its alternative profitable uses). There is also a RISK of financial failure by the client, of a change of government policy or a change of government and of a cash crisis in your own operation.

Progress payments are made for identifiable progress in the project. They can be triggered off by completion of specific stages, from the arrival of the materials for processing, through to delivery on site and fabrication.

Alternative systems include the following.

- Paying up to one-third of the cost of signing the contract.
- Paying one-third at specified stages during the project.
- Paying one-third (less 5%) on completion.
- 5% retained balance is held as a security against unforeseen, or hidden, failings in the structure and an unwillingness on the supplier's part to rectify the problem.

Demand interest on the retained balance.

PROMISE
Best kept.

PROPOSAL
The only thing that can be negotiated. You cannot negotiate an ARGUMENT, a belief, an opinion, a prejudice, a principle, a hope, a GRIEVANCE, a fancy or a fact.

- A proposal is a tentative solution.
- A bargain is a specific conditional OFFER to settle.
- Proposals are best made putting the condition first: if you will do the following, then I am prepared to consider doing such and such.
- If they do not accept your conditions, they cannot have the benefits of your offer.

Proposing discloses information about your settlement range, it being impossible to propose and simultaneously hide your offer. That is why your proposal is specific about what you want them to do, and vague about what you would do in return. The vagueness ("consider", "look at", and so on) loosens your commitment to a specific number or course of action.

Some negotiations require (by statute, custom, necessity, convenience or tactical advantage) that initial proposals be made in writing. These should follow an entry offer format.

- Padded if open to informal negotiation (answering a request for broad details of charges).
- Less padded if open to formal negotiation (approaching an imminent decision or two-offers-only).
- Close to an exit offer if a competitive BID (ONE-OFFER-ONLY).

Verbal proposals have the advantage that you avoid the necessity of revealing your entry point before you have assessed their EXPECTATIONS through constructive debate. They have the dis-advantage that you can fumble the presentation, disclose too much about your PRIORITIES and true ASPIRATIONS (see NON-VERBAL BEHAVIOUR) and make premature CONCESSION exchanges. To obviate these disadvantages, proposals should be:

- stated briefly;
- without long explanations;
- summarised.

Avoid an instant response to a proposal (writ-ten or verbal).
Seek:

- clarification and understanding;
- details of criteria used;
- the thinking behind suggestions.

Do:

- listen to the answers;
- treat each item neutrally;

- summarise your understanding;
- look for bridges between your respective positions;
- consider possibilities for PACKAGING.

PSYCHOLOGY OF NEGOTIATION

The two great drives of human endeavour are our motivations and our cognitive perceptions. These do not always match.

Motivations are best summed up by Maslow's hierarchy of needs which he arranged in an ascending order of importance as each level of need is satisfied.

1 Physiological (hunger, thirst).
2 Safety and security.
3 Love and belonging (acceptance).
4 Self-esteem.
5 Self-actualisation.
6 Knowledge and understanding.
7 Aesthetic.

Experimental and empirical evidence for Maslow's needs, particularly for the higher levels, is mixed. But as a working hypothesis it appears to fit most of the facts.

Physiological. The starving are hardly likely to be concerned about status (unless it is related to access to food), but satisfy the basic needs and the other needs come into play.

For negotiators these needs are important.

Safety and security. A buyer in a new market chooses products that meet his or her security needs (well-known brands, not new ones that might be risky). This is why positioning your product as safe and secure pays off with new buyers entering the market.

Love and belonging. Negotiators with a need to be loved (or respected) are vulnerable. They behave according to what they think is pleasing to whosoever they are with. They try to please everybody. They are no pleasure to deal with.

Either experience improves their performance or they quit the business.

Esteem. Self-esteem, such as the belief that we are worthy because of our professionalism, is a powerful motivator. In negotiating a good deal for our side, or by making the other side work hard for their gains, we become proud of our achievements, especially when set against recognised perceptions of the difficulties involved in achieving what we did. Self-esteem gives us confidence when we negotiate.

Self-actualisation. This comes from demonstrably achieving first class results in a negotiation which stretched us to the limits of our powers. The appeal of a search for excellence finds a response among managers driven by this motivator.

Knowledge. Our cognitive perceptions of the world – the set of beliefs that we work to – have roots that go deep into our psychology, our past, the past of the country we grew up in and our perceptions of the world as adults.

International negotiations are particularly fraught as the cognitive structures of the collective entity known as the nation are not easily or quickly changed. This explains why critics of their country's negotiating stances on certain international issues, who have not themselves sought nor been elected to public office – and thereby have never had to compromise with the public's cognition of these issues – can often see rational "solutions" to these problems and are perplexed at the failure of the government to adopt them. However, in the circumstances these rational solutions are impractical, in the sense that nobody articulating them could get elected.

Aesthetic. Our cognitive disposition includes our prejudices, folk myths and taboos. Negotiating with union representatives also involves negotiating with people imbued with a sense of the (albeit mythical) history of their union.

There is not always a common language accepted by the negotiators.

- "Profit" to a manager may mean "exploitation" and "theft" to a union member.
- "Efficiency" could be perceived as "slave-driving".
- A "good deal" to one negotiator could mean a "rip-off" to another.

Internationally, the paucity of common meanings separates the negotiators of more than one country and political system: consider the different interpretations of the words democracy, justice, rights, welfare, equality and defence found in member states of the United Nations.

There is always a temptation to find contradictions in the cognitive disposition of other negotiators. People are capable of holding passionately to totally contradictory beliefs and to having beliefs that are contradicted by their actions. These intrude into the negotiation as naturally as people blow their noses.

- Attacking somebody's belief system is never successful.
- If a negotiated peace requires the other side to suspend its entire belief system as a first step, there is little hope of success.

Hence consider how to advance your proposals without:

- setting off psychological resistance;
- antagonising or threatening the other negotiators' belief systems;
- undermining their personal motivations.

Instead:

- recognise the legitimacy of the other negotiators' personal motivations;
- refrain from disrespect towards their system of beliefs (no matter how weird you consider their beliefs to be).

Those negotiators who are furthest apart in their cognitive perceptions often find a mutual respect of each other, and this appears to be conducive to reaching a settlement on the practical issues of their relationship when circumstances dictate that such a negotiation is necessary.

PUBLIC STANCE

A COMMITMENT PLOY. By taking a public stance the negotiator signals commitment to the declared outcome, ostensibly putting pressure on the other negotiators. It sometimes works. The other negotiators know that you cannot back off from a public statement without considerable loss of face. This induces them to believe that you intend to fight might and main for your publicly declared OBJECTIVE. In consequence, they give more than they intended.

Alternatively, your public stance imprisons your negotiating flexibility. A reasonable COMPROMISE is excluded because it threatens your public credibility.

Journalists are not given to explanations in public interest stories: either you won or you gave in. Your heroic "statesmanship", your finesse, your brilliantly executed manoeuvre, and so on, are lost in the newspaper headline ("Big Mouth Gives In").

Public stances complicate already complicated disputes. Neither side can move because it has publicly declared that it would not do so.

Agreement is inhibited by public stances. Think carefully before going public on a negotiating objective, especially in response to the other negotiator's public statements.

QUESTIONS

Important advice to all negotiators: ask questions and listen to the answers.

Open questions are better than closed ones. Examples of open questions include the following.

- How did you calculate the rental charge?
- What should I do about office security?
- What suggestions do you have for settling this compensation claim?

Open questions invite the listener to respond with extended statements rather than with yes or no answers.

Examples of closed questions include the following.

- Do you think this policy is fair?
- Are you in favour of an options clause?
- Can you redraw this boundary?

Closed questions are the most common questions yet they are the least effective in securing information. There is not a lot you can do with a yes or no answer. The room for signalling is restricted, and even if the answer is clear – they say "no they do not want it" – you are not told anything about whether some adjustments in the PROPOSAL would satisfy them.

To unblock DEADLOCK, ask open questions. Consider the type of question you are about to ask. You want to get the most detailed and helpful answers that you can, so ask the right questions (content) the right way (open, not closed).

QUESTION NO-NOS

Avoid questions that:

- expose you to mockery;
- expose your ignorance;
- are sarcastic in tone;
- are embarrassing;
- cause trouble;
- are point scoring.

QUESTION THE CRITERIA

Ploy to undermine the other negotiators' PRO-
POSAL. Proposals that are based on facts, rules,
formulae, ASSUMPTIONS, precedents and interpretations of "fairness"' are vulnerable to how they
have been formulated.

- Ask them to explain how they arrived at their
  proposal.
- What data did they use to calculate their
  figures?
- What statement of principle has formed the
  basis of their claim?

Watch out for references to:

- "normal" assessments;
- "standard practice";
- "straightforward" yields;
- "present values";
- "common knowledge".

These could hide phoney assumptions not
applicable in your case.

Compelling the other negotiators to justify their
proposal and its derivation enables you to:

- quibble with their assumptions;
- challenge facts;
- learn something about a market with which
  you are unfamiliar;
- decide on the relevance of their criteria;
- query the reliability of their sources;
- check on the accuracy of their arithmetic;
- question the valuation of intangibles.

Exploring criteria creates negotiating opportunities that were hidden in the plausibility of jargon or assumed expertise.

If you disagree with the criteria the other negotiators have used you have a more defensible
negotiating position than if you accept the criteria
but disagree with the conclusions.

QUICK DEAL
Often regretted.

QUIVERING QUILL
A buyer's pressure ploy. Negotiators close to an
AGREEMENT experience euphoria. The seller is
feeling pleased at the prospect of earning the
value of the deal, perhaps with some of it as a
COMMISSION.

The buyer's pen hovers over the contract. The
seller's anxieties leap upwards: "What do you
mean you need another 2% off the price?"

The buyer puts the pen down and sits back.
Panic in the seller: "Look, if I give you 1% will
you sign now?"

The buyer picks up the pen and leans over the
contract. The quivering quill having quivered,
quivers on. "Make it 1.5% and we have a deal?"
Desperation in the seller: "Okay, okay, just sign
it."

Counter: Same as for YES, BUT. Control your
euphoria until the deal is signed (see PATIENCE).

RAPPORT

Helpful, but not sufficient to secure a negotiated AGREEMENT. Lack of rapport inhibits agreement.

You can help establish rapport by:

- matching your pace to the other negotiators' (particularly across cultures);
- taking a genuine interest in their contribution;
- steering gently towards the settlement you are looking for.

REALISTIC OFFER

An OFFER that can be defended credibly, not one that is fanciful. An offer's credibility is decided by the other negotiator.

- If the other negotiator believes your offer is realistic, then it is realistic.
- Unrealistic offers cause dissent and the other negotiator could break off.
- The further apart you are, the longer it will take to negotiate a solution.
- The other negotiator may be shocked by your offer, but might accept your explanation and adjust his or her own EXPECTATIONS.

RENT

Rentability determines property values. It is what the asset can earn in the MARKET.

If negotiating for the landlord, maximise the net lettable space; if for the tenant, minimise it. The net lettable space is what is usable by the tenant (whether they use it or not). Watch for:

- Measurements running from inside the window alcove to the wall not the skirting board.
- Deductions for central heating apparatus by the walls (when letting, fix a wooden shelf over them and count the space back in).
- How columns in the floor area are treated (if leasing, check that the space they occupy is excluded).

- How stairs, landings and lifts are calculated.
- Charges for common toilets.
- Anywhere showing evidence of use; for example, cabinets in the common areas.

RENT REVIEW

Rent reviews adjust rents to MARKET conditions.

The PRICE per square unit of lettable space is determined by what somebody is willing to pay for it. Be guided by the rents realised in adjacent or similar buildings.

Most rents are for fixed terms which do not coincide with market movements in supply and demand.

The LEASE will include a provision for a rent review at specified dates.

☐ If you are a landlord in a tightening market, impose an "upward only" rent review.

☐ If you are a tenant in a slackening market, delete "upward only".

☐ Landlords should regularly inspect the property to check for chargeable use and to spot misuse.

☐ Tenants should require notice of an inspection to remove evidence of use of uncharged space.

☐ Tenants should research the market for going rates for lettable space.

☐ Tenants should check the earlier measurements of the property in case some structural change has occurred and its rentable implications have been overlooked.

☐ If facing increased rents, tenants should list the defects to TRADE increased rent for repairs.

☐ Landlords can avoid this by imposing full repair and insurance (FRI) terms in the lease, preferably on both an external and internal basis.

Landlords face costs in finding new tenants; tenants face costs in finding new premises. These costs are avoided by negotiating a new AGREEMENT, but they are willingly faced if the offered terms are onerous.

Changes in circumstances are reasons for holding

rents, hence, keep the landlord's letting brochures on file and re-read them before a rent review.

REPUTATION

Lose it and you reduce your opportunities. As your reputation depends on the PERCEPTION of other negotiators and not upon your own, it is easily lost or damaged, sometimes without good cause. What reputation do you want? And with whom?

Establish a negotiating reputation: "This company must establish that it says what it means and means what it says, even if in the short run it costs more than it is worth."

A reputation, once undermined, is less easily put right: it only takes one dispute, where the balance of power is reversed, for a "tough" reputation to crumble in a single retreat.

Interpretation of motives is not an exact science and the same action is judged differently by different negotiators. Being untrustworthy or dishonest damages a reputation, perhaps beyond repair. Deals bypass you, because of your reputation.

RESISTANCE PRICE

The exit OFFER where you prefer "no deal" to a deal on worse terms.

At what PRICE does it become unprofitable to do business? Do not confuse a desirable with a truthful bottom line. You do not know the full facts before you negotiate and circumstances may suggest your original resistance point is unobtainable, but beware that you are not rationalising a surrender under pressure.

Your resistance price may be established arbitrarily by your seniors; beyond this point you get sacked. If it is unrealistic, the time to discuss that is during PREPARATION and not in a post mortem. Think through the implications of and the criteria used to determine your resistance price.

RESTRICTIVE COVENANT

A buyer's protective device. Buyers of businesses protect themselves from future competition by negotiating a restrictive covenant on ex-owners. The ex-owner is prevented from opening a similar business close to the original business. How close is negotiable.

For small businesses, the restrictive covenant bars them from trading within the locality; for national businesses, the restriction may apply to the entire country, or even the world as a whole (although courts have ruled against this).

- The ex-owner may be barred from trading in that business, or one closely related to it, for a fixed term of years.
- The restriction may be confined only to the current clients of the business but permit the ex-owner to generate new business.
- The scope may be narrowly defined (brewing but not barring distribution of beer) or widely defined (design, manufacture, distribution and finance of the product).

Publishers impose highly restrictive covenants on authors which prevent them producing similar works for other publishers that "materially affect the sales of the book", even though they seldom agree not to publish similar books by other authors.

- Some restrictive covenants aim to protect proprietary information, particularly from their research and development personnel.
- Licensors also impose similar conditions on the employees of licensee firms and require the licensee to guarantee protection of the licensor's know-how.

If asked to sign a restrictive covenant, a minimum STRATEGY would be to limit the extent and scope of the restriction and its duration.

REVERSION
A useful clause to protect your INTERESTS in case of default or some failure to meet the contractual obligations by the other negotiators.

Insist that failure to meet obligations, or circumstances such as their bankruptcy, trigger reversion to you of all your rights, property and monies, irrespective of their obligations to others. This is particularly important in a licence AGREEMENT. Liquidators take over property as forfeit in a bankruptcy.

- Make sure that your property unambiguously passes back to you.
- Give notice of reversion immediately you discover failure on the licensee's part to meet the agreed obligations.
- Insert in the agreement that your notice of reversion is unconditionally sufficient for reversion to take effect.

REVIEW

Post-negotiation review of both successful and unsuccessful negotiations is essential to long-term success.

Like PREPARATION, the review should be structured. Use the original preparation plan as the basis for evaluating performance.

☐ How does the negotiated outcome compare with your intentions?
☐ How did the process unfold?
☐ What events were unexpected?
☐ Where in the process do you think you did better/worse than you expected?
☐ What were the main mistakes?
☐ What were the successes?
☐ What was the single most important lesson of the negotiation?

Draw up a list of actions to transform these lessons into improvements in future performance.

RISK

Never eliminated, but it can be reduced or priced. Reduce risk as follows.

- ❑ Seek COLLATERAL.
- ❑ Restrict their discretion.
- ❑ Seek guarantees.
- ❑ Require a PERFORMANCE BOND.
- ❑ Insist on a deposit.
- ❑ Sell or buy forward.
- ❑ Help them count the money.
- ❑ Help them collect it.
- ❑ Factor your invoices.
- ❑ Sell or take an OPTION.
- ❑ Insist on regular payments.
- ❑ Find out what the trouble is and what will put it right.
- ❑ Spread the risk across more than one basket (if you cannot, watch the basket).
- ❑ Calculate income conservatively and costs liberally.
- ❑ Cut your losses.
- ❑ Charge more for the risk.
- ❑ Judge worth by expected value (see DECISION ANALYSIS).

ROYALTIES

Authors get royalties, but few live like royals. They are a percentage share in the retail price of the work, ordinarily about 10% for hardcover books and 7.5% for paperbacks, and then escalating moderately as sales increase.

Authors should follow these guidelines.

- ❑ Require that royalties escalate quickly and the qualifying quantities are reduced.
- ❑ Watch for the "new edition" ploy, that is, the royalty clock re-starts with each new edition. Go for a continuous count.
- ❑ Challenge their estimates of re-setting costs especially if you have supplied the text on disk.
- ❑ Never sell your work for a fixed sum; poor royalties are better than none.

RULES

In negotiation there are none.

What is proper is decided by the negotiators

involved, and even they have no right of "appeal".

Informal "rules" have emerged but they have no status other than what you accord them. For every "rule" there is an exception, and for every negotiator there is a time and circumstance where the "rule" is abandoned.

Some so-called "rules of thumb" might include the following.

☐ Agreements should be honoured.

☐ Sanctions are permissible as complements to the negotiation but not as substitutes.

☐ Solutions should not be imposed on a take-it-or-leave-it basis.

☐ Neither negotiator should interfere in the internal affairs of the other to disrupt their negotiating position or cohesion.

☐ Negotiators should act in "good faith" (*ex bona fide negotiari*) and not behave in a reprehensible and destructive manner.

All these "rules", and many others, are breachable. Often one negotiator abides by one interpretation of a rule and the other by another.

- The alleged "dishonouring" of an AGREEMENT is the subject of many renegotiations.
- At what point a sanction is unacceptable as a negotiating ploy is hotly contested by negotiators.
- Sometimes "take-it-or-leave-it" is all that is left when faced with obstinacy.
- Negotiators interfere in each other's affairs – that is what propaganda, public stances, leaks, rumours and threats are all about – to weaken the opposing coalition.
- Courts and arbitration sittings are full of disputes about "good faith".

RUSSIAN FRONT

A ploy to make you accept one unpalatable option by forcing you to choose between two unpalatable options, with one of them so unpalatable that you opt for the lesser one.

It is an allusion to the effect on soldiers of threats of being sent to the "Russian front" in the second world war from "B" movies. If the officer had the power to send someone to the Russian front, he could exact compliance with his wishes. The soldier cringed: "No, no, anything but the Russian front."

For example:

Q: Either you send me a list of the ten least efficient people to be made redundant in your operation, or I will assume that it doesn't matter who is made redundant (including yourself) and I will sack ten people at random.
A: Do you want the list typed or can I name them now?

SALAMI

"A slice of a cut sausage will not be missed." And it is not. Can you package your conditional PRO-POSAL using a salami?

Children use salami. You tell them not to go out of your sight in the park. They move away but stay in sight. Then they sit on the ground and you have to strain your neck to see them. Then they lie down, so you have to get up to see them. They slide down the slope out of sight, but return every few minutes in case you are checking on them. Sometimes you see them, sometimes you do not, but they return enough times to stop you worrying too much, and anyway, you are getting tired jumping up and down to look for them. Then they go off for longer spells. You fret. They are off for an adventure but come back, eventually. They salamied you.

SANCTION

Any measure aimed to coerce the other party. Sanctions include the following.

Employee relations

- Go-slows.
- Overtime bans.
- Strikes.
- Working to rule.
- Discriminating against identifiable groups.
- Worktime meetings.
- Refusing duty.
- Withholding necessary consents, documents, formal requirements.
- Occupying places of work to prevent others working.
- Picketing.
- Banning specified inputs.
- Refusing to work "blacked" materials.
- Imposing bans of any kind.
- Rigorously applying safety rules.
- Mislaying materials, papers, information.
- Sabotage.
- Withdrawing special cover (safety, security).

- Sympathetic actions of any kind in support of other disputes.
- Clogging up the disputes procedures with spurious cases.
- Prolonging meetings to waste time.
- Refusing to meet.
- Making public statements on confidential matters.

Commercial relations

- Cancelling contracts.
- Returning work unfinished.
- Holding on to drawings.
- Litigation.
- Calling in loans.
- Changing suppliers.
- Withholding consents.
- Mislaying necessary documents.
- Returning work on trivial technical grounds.
- Refusing to pay invoices.
- Holding up payments on one contract while there is a dispute on another contract.
- Refusing to maintain equipment.
- Withdrawing supplies except on onerous or cash terms.
- Calling a creditors' meeting.
- Appointing a receiver.
- Reporting alleged offences to an official agency, professional body or the general public.
- Withdrawing financial support.
- Liquidating the business.
- Selling shares.
- Placing votes in a shareholders' meeting.
- Not electing directors, sacking employees, including directors.

Trade relations

- Discriminatory trade practices.
- Quotas.
- Tariffs and non-tariff burdens.
- Selective import controls.

- Withholding export guarantees.
- Restricting or banning investment.
- Selective and general trade sanctions.
- Dumping.
- Using vetoes in international organisations.
- Administrative delays.
- Embargoes.

International relations

- Withholding support in public.
- Working behind the scenes to withhold support.
- Making public condemnations.
- Joining in coalitions to oppose specific INTERESTS.
- Blockades.
- Using military force at any level, including war.
- Taking hostages.
- Taking punitive action against specific citizens.
- Terrorism.

SECONDARY BOYCOTT
A coercive measure used by unions, presently illegal in the USA and the UK. Sympathy strikes in unrelated businesses to put pressure on an employer.

SEEKING CLARIFICATION
Proposals are not always clearly stated. Clarification is essential if you are unclear, and bridge-building even if you are. People like to be treated seriously. Asking clarification QUESTIONS helps to build rapport.

Q: Could you go over the second clause? I am not sure how you intend it to operate.
Q: Am I right in thinking that your liability clause would cover us up to two years from installation?

Questions sometimes finesse explanations that provide additional information about their wants and PRIORITIES. They can lead on to criteria questions.

SELL AND LEASE BACK

A way to raise capital on your assets.

Lenders supply funds against first-class assets, such as prime site properties. You receive the capital for other purposes and lease the properties you formerly owned. Sometimes there are tax regimes that are favourable to these deals.

This could be attractive to a takeover bidder who wants to release funds from the acquired company to reduce borrowings without damaging the income-earning capacity of the business. In the short term the target for the takeover pays for you taking it over. The disadvantage is that you lose control of your properties, and can face rising rents at any subsequent RENT REVIEW.

You could place the company's properties into a separate property company, which then borrows against its property and pays off the borrowings out of rents it charges the main company for use of the properties. The loan is secured against the property company's assets and cash is released for other purposes. When the mortgages are repaid the company still owns its properties.

SELL CHEAP, GET FAMOUS

A buyer's ploy. Anybody new to a business has no track record. Newcomers cannot attract the premiums that go with experience. Buyers exploit this opportunity. The ploy persuades newcomers to accept a lower price for their services.

Buyer: How many plants of this type have you designed?
Newcomer: This is my first contract.
Buyer: How many times have you been consulted about this type of business problem?
Newcomer: I did something similar in my MBA course.

The buyer is softening you up for a low fee pitch. But he (or she) does not just push you down on price, he makes out he is doing you a favour.

- Design this plant for the fee I have suggested, and you will establish your reputation and earn big fees on all subsequent work.
- Invest in solving this problem and you will soon be quoting with the big league consultants.

You sell yourself cheap to recoup the situation in future business. Some people, finding it hard to get started, offer their services free to clients just to get a track record.

Counter: With difficulty, if your track record is a blank sheet of paper. If forced to accept a lower opening fee (do not fall for the "get famous" bit), go for a version of the contingency ADD-ON:

- If the design is accepted, then you pay me a second fee of 30%.
- If my solution is adopted, you pay me another $5,000.

SHAM OFFER
Using an entry OFFER to disguise your TARGET. You open with a sham offer of $400, leaving room to TRADE back to your target price of $380. Your exit price is $360. Opening at your target forces you to trade below it, which mocks your concept of a target.

If they accept your sham offer, apply the ADD-ON.

SHOCK OPENING
An abrasive pressure ploy.

The other negotiators open with a price that is wildly outside your EXPECTATIONS. You are shocked into stunned surprise. If they follow through with a credible reason for their proposal you have to review your expectations.

The key requirement for a shock opening is credibility. The other negotiators, hearing a shock opening, are forced to reconsider the basis of their own position. "Perhaps our price is too high?"

Even if the shock opening only moves the other negotiators part of the way from their expectations towards yours, your opening shock has been effective. There is a risk, however, that you are so far away from their expectations that they break off the negotiations.

SHUT UP

Silence: there is not a lot of it about. Add to what there is by LISTENING more than you talk. Why? Because you know what is in your mind but you do not know what is in theirs. You will not find out by talking.

Shut up immediately after you:

- make a PROPOSAL;
- summarise;
- ask a question;
- reach an AGREEMENT.

Wait until they respond before you speak again.

Shut up when you have nothing to say. You do not have to fill every silence with your words. Let the power of silence put pressure on them.

SIGNAL

Subtle change in a negotiator's language, indicating a willingness to consider movement.

- What is "impossible" becomes "difficult".
- What was "never done" becomes "not normally done".
- What was "contrary to company policy" becomes "without precedent or prejudice".
- What was "no way" becomes "not under current circumstances".

Without signals negotiators would have considerable difficulty in moving without giving the impression that they were about to surrender. Everybody signals – most people do not realise that they are signalling – but many negotiators miss signals because they are not LISTENING.

Some negotiators punish the signaller: "I see, so you are no longer holding to your ludicrous opening OFFER?" This drives them back to ARGUMENT, and delays a settlement. Do not punish a signal. Question it for clarification, encourage the other negotiator to elaborate.

Q: You say you have a difficulty with my request. Is there any way that I could make it easier for you to meet my needs?
Q: Under what conditions would your company be willing to make an ex gratia payment in circumstances like mine?

Signals are normally a prelude to a PROPOSAL, and no negotiation can get very far without proposals.

SIZZLE

"Do not sell the steak, sell the sizzle." The world's most successful selling technique, developed by Elmer Wheeler, who believed that "the heart is closer to the pocket book than is the brain".

Find the sizzle in a proposition and put that to them. It goes down better than dry facts. It breaks through their INHIBITIONS.

In a competitive MARKET why should an exporter ship with you rather than anybody else? Give a reason: "Do not sell cargo space (all your competitors have space), sell guaranteed delivery."

Why should a bank choose your firm to liquidate a business? Do not sell accountancy knowledge (competing accountants have that too), sell a hassle-free liquidation.

Counter: When buying, "buy the steak, not the sizzle".

SKIMMER

Somebody who gets between you and the deal, and insists on being "taken care of" before the deal progresses much further. In some countries they pop out of the woodwork unexpectedly. They wait until the contractor is chosen and then get between the contractor and the client. That way they get paid off, no matter which of you wins the contract. Their position (perhaps a connection with the ruling family, perhaps a crucial role in the final decision) guarantees their ability to frustrate the deal. You pay up, or get nowhere.

Sometimes you can block skimmers by making a fuss with their boss, though the skimmer could be working for the boss, who prefers not to sully his reputation with an open demand for a bribe.

Try PADDING the PRICE with the skimmer's pay-off if the approach is made before you get to price. If the price is set – that is why you got the contract – the skimmer's (large) fee comes out of your profit.

Beware of people who claim to be able to block your deal but who are in fact only charming chancers. Pay them and you cut your profits, and if the real skimmers turn up, demanding their share of the cake, you are going to be working for nothing.

SKIMMING

A pricing STRATEGY. Some people are PRICE-blind when it comes to new products. They want the very best and expect to pay for it (if you do not go in high they think your product is a cheapie).

Luxury cars, yachts, electronic gadgets, new products of all kinds, are ripe for a price-skimming strategy. The MARKET is limited, deliberately so, but it is lucrative until the competition starts up (they see your pricey products and the people with money wanting to buy them).

Skim the "cream" with the high-price strategy, then expand output and lower prices gradually, as you work your way into the next segment of customers who want the product but are more price-sensitive than the people at the "top end".

SKINNER'S PIGEON

Professor B.F. Skinner of Harvard University claimed that human beings could be conditioned into behaviour patterns given the right stimulus and reward system. The professor demonstrated his theory by training a pigeon to pick out the ace of spades from a deck of cards, no matter how they were shuffled.

The lesson for negotiators is to consider the relative size of the brains of a pigeon and a human negotiator (roughly a pea to a cabbage). If a pigeon can learn to choose the ace of spades, how much cleverer is a human being learning from the behaviour of another negotiator?

Negotiators learn to say no if they find they get concessions when they do so, hence do not stimulate their resistance by rewarding it.

SOFTNESS

Soft negotiators are characterised by their willingness to move in large steps from any position they adopt. Their basic fear is that of not securing an AGREEMENT. They:

- almost prefer any agreement to DEADLOCK;
- negotiate with themselves;
- crumble under threats;
- have an extensive repertoire for rationalising acceptance of any agreement offered;
- tend, also, to talk too much;
- qualify any (often unconditional) OFFER they make with a SIGNAL of how far they are prepared to move if it is not acceptable.

SPLIT THE DIFFERENCE

A settlement ploy. Negotiators stuck on two numbers can move to a settlement by "splitting the difference". You offer $80, they offer $40; splitting the difference gives you $60.

It sounds fair and equitable and sometimes it is. It can also be expensive; perhaps you cannot afford to split the difference?

To avoid its being sprung on you stick to numbers that do not have an obvious split point. If your offer is $83.5 and theirs is $40 it is not obvious what number splits the difference, and that which is not obvious is not so "fair" as that which is.

An offer to split the difference is risky because you disclose a willingness to move 50% of the difference between you. The other negotiators could exploit your SIGNAL and refuse to move, leaving you with a more difficult task in defence of your original number. They could also offer a different split: "I cannot go 50:50, but I will consider 30:70."

When an obvious split point emerges – you have proposed 10% and they have replied with 8% – move to bury the obvious split point by offering 9.85% (conditionally).

If the difference is trivial, there are bigger issues at stake and your relationship with the other negotiators justifies it, agree to split the difference as part of a larger package but not in isolation.

STANDARD TERMS
Alibi for loading the contract terms against you.

Sellers often print their terms and conditions on the reverse of their official letters confirming an order, or they are printed on their order forms which they expect you to sign. These standard terms always restrict their liabilities and are onerous to you, not to them, which is why they are printed.

Read them carefully. If you cannot accept them all, acknowledge their order in writing with a reference that it is accepted subject to your terms (enclosed), or to the exclusion of their specific term (reference number only). They may be so desperate to receive your goods that they waive their own terms. Later, they could change their minds but they are unable to enforce them once waived.

Printed terms are intimidating. They imply that they cannot be changed (which is why they are often printed close together, so that changes are near impossible). To avoid signing an official order form with its specific terms, send them an order in writing with your terms on it.

Standard terms are negotiable, but only if you take the trouble to query them.

STRATEGIC INTERACTION

Jargon from GAME THEORY which describes how negotiators manipulate the information they pass to each other.

You do not know what is going on in the heads of the other negotiators. They are less than candid about their predicament because you might exploit this information. They think how you are likely to react to their behaviour knowing that this is a reaction to your behaviour; how you think they think you think they think you think. . . Taken too far, concern with strategic interaction paralyses the negotiators into infinite regresses.

STRATEGY

Best kept simple. Complicated strategies fail within a few moves because the other negotiators have not read your script; they have a different plan.

The strategy is dependent on the circumstances and the issues in the negotiation. Not mentioning money, for example, might be a strategic objective when the value of what is for sale is not obvious (neither negotiator knows for certain the other negotiator's valuation). By keeping money in the background until they have ascertained enough information to set the "PRICE" the negotiators prevent an early "over" or "under" price being established.

Strategy should be flexible: if it is not working do not persist. It should also be linked to your marketing and pricing plans.

But, above all, remember what Robert Burns said about the "best laid plans of mice and men".

STRESS

Negotiating is a stressful activity. You are:

* anxious about the outcome;
* emotional about their behaviour;
* unsure of the implications of offers;
* worried about their intentions;
* concerned about not doing as well as you, or your peers, expect.

Stress cannot be eliminated; it can be reduced. The professional negotiator tries:

- not to take things personally;
- to separate the issues from the personalities;
- to concentrate on INTERESTS rather than issues.

Basically, you should slow down the pace (ask more QUESTIONS), relax before and after sessions, and set realistic rather than fanciful targets.

STRIKE

Withdrawing labour is a legal right of employees.

Strikes aim to influence negotiation. The strike can be a prelude to a negotiated settlement or a substitute for one. Strikes over highly contentious issues are bitterly fought.

The strategy of the strikers is to prevent normal business being conducted. The strategy of the employer is to ensure that normal, or near normal, business continues.

If the strikers succeed in stopping normal business, it is a matter of resource attrition: which side runs out of resources first? If the company succeeds in continuing with normal business, it is a matter of TIME pressure: how long before the strikers give up?

Public relations are important in strikes.

- Denouncing strikers as "extremists" when they manifestly are not is counter-productive.
- People who strike before exhausting the opportunities for negotiation are in a weaker position than those who are driven to strike by the intransigence of the employers.
- Avoid being provoked into a strike; you might not be as indispensable as you think.
- Companies which make public statements about the "damage" done by, or the costs of, the strike strengthen the strikers (they feel they are achieving something).
- Strikes that appear likely to last a long time are over more quickly than those that appear

to be short-term (hence, if asked how long you can take the strike, answer: "indefinitely").

Handling "peace" talks is difficult. Public stances and reports of what is happening are unhelpful.

- If talks fail avoid shrill denunciations of the other negotiators: the calm acceptance of failure, in sorrow not anger, wins more votes in the public relations war. It also makes it easier for talks to recommence when they are willing to have another go.
- Employers should open the plants to employees who want to work if the strike is a substitute for negotiation.
- If you co-operate in closing down your operation with the strikers you will enhance the authority of the strike leaders over your employees, which is contrary to your INTERESTS.

"SUBJECT TO BOARD APPROVAL"

You have been negotiating with the monkeys, not the organ grinders. There is always an organ grinder on the board who thinks he (or she) could do better than the monkeys, and he demonstrates his superiority by sending the AGREEMENT back with his amendments.

Counter: Pad offers that are subject to board approval.

SUMMARISING

Simple but effective negotiating behaviour.

Negotiations are chaotic. The verbal interaction wanders. People join the flow of conversation and set it off at a tangent (or back to something already covered). Interruptions occur, both planned and unplanned. A summary refocuses attention on to the issues.

- What has been said about them.
- What each side is proposing.

- What the differences are.
- What remains to be agreed.
- What has been agreed.

Summaries should be short (they are a summary not a blow-by-blow account) and neutral (cover each side's point of view and what they have proposed).

A biased summary can start an ARGUMENT. A neutral summary placed in the middle of a long bout of verbiage, or at the moment when the debate is wandering off into unhelpful territory, can work wonders on even the most jaded or hot-tempered of negotiators.

Summarise during all phases of the negotiation, particularly:

- when argument is dominating the exchanges;
- immediately after your PROPOSAL;
- when calling for agreement;
- after agreement has been reached, to check that what you think you have agreed corresponds to what they believe.

SWITCH SELLING

A seller's ADD-ON tactic. You think you are negotiating to buy a deluxe model widget, but you find yourself being sold the super deluxe model. The seller has "switch sold" you up the range.

Sometimes this is to your benefit – the super deluxe is really more suited to your needs – but often it is not. They advertise a fantastic bargain. When you get there they have sold out of the "bargain", but they do have a few "slightly more expensive" versions available.

Counter: Insist it is the original deal or no deal.

TABLE

Like the VENUE, if it matters to one of you, it matters to both of you.

Negotiators like to sit behind a table, and not just to lay their papers or elbows on it. It is partly instinctive: a table "protects" you in the same way that you use your legs and arms to cover parts of your body when you feel threatened or unsure (see NON-VERBAL BEHAVIOUR).

Negotiations begin in conflict (your solution or mine) and end in co-operation (a jointly agreed solution). Putting something between you and them reassures your subconscious anxieties. If you did not feel comfortable you would perform less well, even display overt antagonism.

Some experts, confusing cause for consequence, think you should force negotiators to sit next to each other in an "open" formation because they believe that tables exacerbate conflict.

TACIT BARGAINING

Where communication is not possible, or extremely circumscribed, and the parties make their moves on how they expect the other party to behave, or in reaction to how they perceive them to be behaving (see PRISONER'S DILEMMA).

In competition with a rival firm, you have a choice of increasing your PRICE or maintaining it (perhaps costs are rising and squeezing profits for both of you). As collusion between suppliers is illegal you face ruinous price competition, but through tacit bargaining you "agree" to raise prices, in the knowledge that your rival will follow and not exploit your move, so that you both profit.

TAKE-OFF

Reverse of the ADD-ON. A ploy to raise your PRICE safely, or when a buyer challenges your price and you have padded it.

You quote a price that covers your costs plus add-ons.

Seller: My normal price for this service is $700.
Buyer: That is far too high, and way outside our budget.

Take off a little.

Seller: You realise I have included my travel expenses in the price.
Buyer: A bit better, but still . . .

Take off some more.

Seller: Plus my hotel expenses.
Buyer: I see.

You have entered the settlement range.

The take-off enables you to raise your price safely. If challenged you retreat a little. If unchallenged apply the add-on: add your expenses on top of the $700.

TARGET

The negotiating OBJECTIVE you aim to reach if you can. It is what you want to settle on.

If you open at your target you are likely to be forced to move away from it, unless they accept your FIRST OFFER.

TAXATION

An avoidable, but not evadable cost. If tax collectors believe that:

- you owe them money in a clear-cut case;
- legal precedent and legislation are beyond doubt;
- you can pay it;

they issue an instruction to pay and you pay up, subject to your right of appeal.

You can arrange payment terms with their consent, but you cannot demand them if you have:

- been caught evading payment;
- obstructed their investigations;
- prevaricated and used outright deceit.

You probably face a prison sentence too.

The tax collectors' interest is in collecting as much taxation as the law prescribes (personal promotion and salaries depend on it). Thus, where the legal issues are complicated (nobody has devised an unambiguous tax system yet) and the outcome of an appeal to the courts is uncertain, the tax authorities are usually willing to negotiate how much you pay and when you pay it, in order to collect something for certain as opposed to an uncertain amount later, and to avoid the risk of losing the case and letting others know of the loophole you found (tax cases are widely publicised).

TEACHING WOLVES TO CHASE SLEDGES

Often futile concessions to generate goodwill.

You are under pressure. The other negotiator is challenging you hard on PRICE; you think the best way to relieve the pressure is to concede something small. You do so. Nothing happens. The pressure continues so you concede something more with the same result. You are perplexed.

You ought not to be. Your behaviour is creating the pressure not relieving it. If you concede in the face of pressure, you teach other negotiators to pile on the pressure.

It is like trying to discourage wolves from chasing your sledge by throwing food to them. This does not work because you are teaching them that if they want to be fed, they should chase sledges.

TEAMWORK

It has advantages and disadvantages. Both can be optimised by PREPARATION and discipline.

The leader carries the bulk of the burden of conducting the negotiation and must make the tactical decisions and call the shots. People not directly involved can slip into the role of spectators, which, as any player will tell you, leads to them assume they can do better. They are tempted into interventions, not always well-timed and, in the extreme, they attempt coups d'états.

- Teams must be disciplined. The only appropriate time and place for criticism and dissent is in a private ADJOURNMENT, not in front of the other negotiators.

- Who should be the leader? It is appropriate for the leader to be the best-qualified person, irrespective of seniority.

- What do the other members of the team contribute? If there is no obvious answer, why are they there? A lot of TIME is taken up with negotiation, and people who are not needed should do something more productive.

- Forming teams solely to match the other team's numbers is not very sensible. A well-briefed team need not be the same size as the other side's. There is no "safety in numbers", only expense.

- Somebody SUMMARISING is a great help to the leader. Summaries provide well-needed breaks, reduce tension, refocus the negotiations on the issues and demonstrate that you are LISTENING to what the other negotiators are saying.

- Experts and specialists can be consulted or invited to contribute on narrowly defined lines to the discussions. If technical issues are central to the negotiation, have people present who can contribute sensibly but ensure that they are commercially minded. Once technical people start drifting into technicalities they can destroy a commercial negotiating position. Interactions between your experts and those on the other side should be restricted.

- You often need an observer. It is always "easier" to analyse a negotiation from the observer's position than it is if you are contributing to what is going on. Adjournments give opportunities for the observer to contribute to the assessment of the state of play and to make recommendations for future actions.

- Teams should always prepare together. Unbriefed or partially briefed team members are dangerous allies.

TERMINATION

Essential clause in a contract. A specified date for the termination of the current contract covers you against a perpetual contract that contains, because circumstances change, onerous consequences.

THOUSAND EXCEPTIONS

A ploy to weaken the implementation of a policy.

Attacking a policy head-on is not always fruitful. The momentum behind it is so great that it sweeps all before it. The thousand exceptions is a reverse SALAMI: instead of helping to introduce a policy by restricting its immediate application, you help undermine a policy by limiting its application.

Any policy is vulnerable when its practical details are considered. A general implementation could be limited by the sheer administrative cost of applying it everywhere at once.

❐ Discover awkward exceptions.

❐ Create exceptions.

❐ List exceptions.

❐ Do not indicate your total opposition to the theme of the policy (which its supporters would latch on to and isolate immediately).

The more committed you appear to be to the policy, the more convincing your "regret" that "unfortunately, for the moment, and with current resources, it would be wiser to confine it to this limited application".

THREAT

Unlike a promise, something that you prefer not to implement.

Threats are part of the repertoire of COERCION. There are two kinds.

- Compliance. Unless you do the following specific things, we will do the following to you.
- Deterrence. If you do the following things, we will do the following to you.

The consequences of a compliance threat can be avoided by doing what the threatener requires. Examples include threats to:

- strike unless the company pays higher wages;
- attack unless a country withdraws its forces;
- leave unless your partner stops drinking.

The consequences of a deterrence threat can be avoided by refraining from doing what the threatener objects to. Examples include threats to:

- use force if you attack them;
- strike if you sack employees;
- leave if your partner starts drinking.

Threats are judged on:

- the capability of the threateners to carry out the threat;
- the likelihood of them doing so if thwarted in their other intentions;
- their likely effects if they are implemented.

Threats raise the tension of a negotiation. A threat cycle is difficult to stop. People do not like to be threatened because, apart from the disagreeable consequences to them of the threats being implemented, they do not like to have their choices circumscribed. If they comply/desist it appears they did so because of the threat, thus encouraging more threats, when they may, for other reasons, wish to adopt a course of action, or inaction, which corresponds to the threatener's preferences.

Threats may achieve their aims without being implemented, or they may not be believed and have to be implemented or withdrawn. A threat that achieves its ends without being implemented could be the result of a tactical adjustment by the other negotiators who are temporarily unable under existing conditions to resist the threat. But as soon as those conditions change, they seek revenge.

- Making specific threats is more convincing than being vague, but it is also more restrictive for the threatener. If the threat is ignored, the threatener has little choice but to implement the threat or lose credibility.

- Private threats are more likely to succeed than public ones. If those threatened resent the public loss of face in succumbing to the threat, they might feel compelled to refuse to budge and force the threat to be implemented.
- Vague threats leave the initiative to the threatener as to whether, or how, the threats are implemented, but the vaguer they are the less convincing they become.
- Bluffing threats are risky because they might be called (loss of credibility). If you must bluff, be vague in your intentions, as this gives room for doubt about what triggers the threat's implementation. If those threatened suspect or believe (intelligence, own assessment of the situation) that you are bluffing they could call your bluff and you could end up in a war or strike even though originally you were bluffing.

TIME

The great pressuriser. Negotiations fill the time available, and if that is less than planned for, the negotiator either moves faster more frequently or blows it.

Time pressure:

- is uncomfortable;
- adds stress to an already stressful situation;
- forces hard choices;
- can split a negotiating team apart, because their perceptions of what is now possible do not change at the same rate.

Time can be compressed (we decide by 5pm) or extended (we will call you when we have considered all the proposals). In the former the negotiators are racing the clock, in the latter they are watching it.

Negotiators working against time prefer to

postpone the other negotiators' making a decision until they have had a full chance to influence that decision.

Negotiators kicking their heels waiting for a decision rapidly reach the point where they do not care what decision it is as long as it is a decision.

Counters:

- Have more than one time plan for a negotiation (a long one and a short one) and be ready to work to whichever plan suits the time that becomes available.
- Maintain strong communication links between the negotiators and the home base, including regular briefings if possible.
- Adapt the negotiators to the time climate by sending in support if the negotiation is compressed (do not leave it to stressful meetings of pressurised team members), or by pulling out people if they can be used elsewhere while fully supporting those who are left.

TIT-FOR-TAT

A WIN-WIN strategy. Robert Axelrod showed how the best STRATEGY for an indefinite run of dilemma plays is for the players to adopt tit-for-tat. A player co-operates on the first move and from then on does whatever the other player did on the previous move.

The strategy "teaches" the other players that the benefits from co-operation are available if they choose a co-operative OPTION (because you always respond positively), but that if they choose to defect, so will you. As the rewards to each from co-operation over the long run are greater than the rewards for defection (because defection is always punished), they have a strong incentive to co-operate.

Signalling co-operation without being exploited is the most difficult task facing a negotiator. Tit-for-tat is a workable strategy because it is obvious what you are up to and it is simpler than the alternatives.

It works best when the negotiators take a long-term view of the relationship. Short-term gains can overwhelm intentions to co-operate, even though the negotiators know this is irrational in the long run.

When playing tit-for-tat:

- never defect first;
- if the other negotiator defects react immediately – you have a low threshold to provocation;
- remember that a delayed response weakens your signalled message.

If they decide to co-operate again:

- forgive them for their defection without rancour;
- immediately respond co-operatively;
- do not exact additional punishment "just to show them". Your objective is to bring them to their senses, not to their knees.

TOUGH GUY/NICE GUY

A ploy which works best on frightened negotiators. It is an act: two negotiators alternate between a tough, uncompromising, highly aggressive and COMPETITIVE STYLE, and a softer, more CO-OPERATIVE STYLE.

Naturally you prefer to deal with the apparently softer person, but his (or her) "hands are tied" by his tougher colleague. He wants to help you but he needs you to help him. So you move closer to his position than you intended, but you are comforted by the illusion that this is a lot less far than you would have had to go to satisfy the "gorilla" who did all the shouting and made all those impossible demands.

You have been had. The duet was a set-up to make you concede. Neither is nicer or nastier than the other. They compare notes afterwards, and laugh all the way to the next negotiation.

TOUGHNESS

Much misunderstood. Tough negotiators:

- Aim for the TARGET, having made proper preparations beforehand.
- Are not afraid of DEADLOCK and do not give up easily.
- Open with a REALISTIC OFFER and move modestly.
- Listen carefully to what the other negotiators say.
- Closely scrutinise all the details of what the other party wants.
- Only move conditionally (if you . . . then I . . .).

TRADABLES

The currency of the BARGAINING process. They cover anything, tangible or intangible, over which either party has discretion.

Movement is secured by offering to TRADE something that you have for something that they have.

Common tradables include the following.

- Money: PRICE, wages, finance, currency, credit, profits, income, taxes, bonds.
- Time: when it happens, who to, who from.
- Goods: quantities, quality, features, substitutes.
- Specification: marginal changes, performance standards.
- Services: standards, personnel, performance.
- Guarantees: guarantor, liability, liquidated damages.
- Warranties: duration, extent, coverage.
- RISK: extent, who carries it, shares.

Considering the tradables available to you as a negotiator gives you ideas for PREPARATION, for new strategies, new proposals, new ways to get out of DEADLOCK.

TRADE

Never give an inch: trade it. Trading constitutes the singular difference of negotiation compared with other forms of decision-making. What is traded may be:

- tangible or intangible;
- something in the present or a promise of something in the future;
- of value to both or only to one of the negotiators.

Trade involves exchange. One negotiator gives up something he or she has, or controls, or can promise for the future, in exchange for something the other negotiator has, controls or can promise.

Negotiation is about the terms of the trade: how much is given in exchange for how much is received.

TRADE UNION

An employee's bargaining AGENT. In theory, most are run by their members; in practice, they are run by small minorities of "active" members. The quality of elections and decision-making processes varies widely. Some members are fiercely loyal to the union, while most blow hot and cold depending on circumstance. It rarely pays to make membership of the union an issue, unless it has gone over the top with serious misbehaviour (such as intimidation, political strikes).

TRUST

Earned not deserved. Trust is unlikely to flourish when the negotiators are:

- suspicious of motives, intentions, capabilities or past behaviour;
- hostile for any reason;
- highly competitive;
- contesting vital issues;
- facing big gains or losses;
- feeling threatened;
- ignorant of each other;
- recent victims of trickery.

Trust flourishes when the negotiators have:

- demonstrated their reliability;
- experience of each other in a variety of

circumstances;

- invested in confidence-building measures;
- reciprocated in helpful ways and not taken unfair advantage when they could have.

Does trust pay off? Not if its consequences are assumed without being tested. To trust someone recklessly is as risky as dealing with someone who is totally untrustworthy.

If trust is earned by being of proved quality, it pays off handsomely. WIN-WIN outcomes are easier to arrive at if the negotiators are able to be open about their needs without fear of being exploited.

Mutual trust enables the negotiators to increase the size of the cake by exploring, in a safe atmosphere, new solutions to difficult problems.

UNCONDITIONAL OFFER

Music to the ears of the other negotiators. An unconditional offer is a wasted offer. The other negotiators will accept the offer but come back for more. One-way conceding is no way to conduct a negotiation. Make conditional offers.

USED-CAR SALE

A classic example of DISTRIBUTIVE BARGAINING. Neither you nor the seller knows the other's exit PRICE, nor whether the first price mentioned is a SHAM OFFER or a TARGET price.

Treat a FIRST OFFER as an offer that can be improved upon. Whatever they open with, no matter how good it looks alongside your target and exit prices, HAGGLE. Convince sellers that:

- they prefer a sale on terms more favourable to you than they originally expected to get;
- your terms for the car are less favourable to them than they expect;
- a quick certain sale to you now at a lower price than they want is better for them than waiting for another customer;
- you will settle at once if the price is right.

All positive comments on the vehicle's characteristics, or the maker's reputation, or your need for it, undermine your stance.

Sellers ask early on what price range you are interested in. They are assessing your exit price, not saving you time looking through their range. So do not tell them. Ask to see their cars. Once sellers have invested time in trying to sell you a car, they are even keener to come to a deal.

❑ Take up their time.
❑ Ask QUESTIONS.
❑ Keep them waiting while you go over every inch of the vehicle.
❑ Don't show keenness for a particular vehicle.
❑ Let them revise downwards their likely profit in order to close the deal.

VALUING CONCESSIONS

It is not what it is worth to you that counts, but what it is worth to the other negotiators.

The temptation to give things away that are of little value to ourselves is universal. Value everything in the other negotiators' terms. Ask yourself: "What is it worth to them? If they want it, then they value it, and if they value it, what can I get back from them that I value?"

Negotiating is decision-making by trading. You TRADE things that are cheaper for you, but valued by the other negotiator, for things that are valued by you, but cheaper for the other negotiator.

VENUE

Where the negotiations take place is occasionally important to one or both negotiators. A home venue might be advantageous to one of the parties.

- They control the environment.
- They can manipulate the HOSPITALITY.
- They are closer to their coalition members whom they can consult.
- They have access to records, files and data.
- They are visibly "in charge".

However, one party's advantage is not necessarily another party's disadvantage.

- They cannot walk out of their own premises.
- They cannot claim to have AUTHORITY, if the people with the alleged authority are nearby.
- Any failures in the services to the negotiation, or any embarrassments, are more likely to undermine the composure of the hosts than the guests.

When negotiating at the client's premises there is the problem of the security of your recess rooms and communications with your head office. If premature disclosure of your views on the situation is likely to undermine your position, you have fewer remedies on their home ground than you do on yours.

In dictatorships there are no neutral venues, and you can take it for granted that surveillance goes on irrespective of your status (they spy on each other, so what is so special about you?).

What are you looking for in an ideal venue?

☐ Good size negotiating room with space to walk about and work in comfort.

☐ Comfortable furniture, lighting and ventilation.

☐ Recess rooms for each team, with direct-dial and secure telephones and access to fax.

☐ Discreet venue staff who go about their work quietly and do not interfere in events.

☐ Everything cleaned and tidied during breaks, and all refreshments replenished regularly.

VULNERABILITY

Ask yourself where you are vulnerable in a business situation. It might help you to protect your flanks from surprises. For example:

- A short-term lease leaves you vulnerable to a notice to quit when it is least convenient.
- A long-term lease might bind you in when you see better opportunities elsewhere.

These considerations prompt you to cover your vulnerability in your PROPOSAL.

- A management is vulnerable just before an order surge arrives: the employees might take advantage of the pressure to extract concessions.
- An absent partner is vulnerable to decisions made without him or her.
- A supplier is vulnerable to competition offering similar lines.
- We are all vulnerable to accidents.

Thinking about vulnerabilities is productive if it produces constructive measures to avert being ambushed when least expected or welcomed.

WAKING UP THE DEAD

A risky intervention ploy. Faced with determined negotiators and not making much progress, it is tempting to try to explore differences of view in their team. You invite a member of the other team who has remained silent throughout the session to comment.

- What do you think, Mr Sujamo?
- Have you any suggestions about how to break this impasse, Ms Allbright?

You are taking a RISK. The other negotiators might resent your interference and retaliate by stiffening their position. If the team is disciplined, you are unlikely to succeed.

WALK-OUT

It does not always work. They do not come running after you; they leave you to stew.

- Are you walking out to signal your total disapproval of something they have said, suggested, done or implied?
- Can you demonstrate disapproval in some other way?
- Why not tell them what you feel?
- What do you do when you are faced with a walk-out by the other negotiators?

As a pressure ploy it lacks a focus because it is not clear what the other negotiators are meant to do when you walk out. The other team might believe that you are serious about your stance and accommodate you but they might also regard you as unstable.

If it is a COLLECTIVE BARGAINING dispute, a diplomatic problem, or a spouse argument, the walk-out might bring things to a head, though not necessarily in the way you intended (they wanted you to strike, to DEADLOCK, to abandon the matrimonial home, and so on).

How do you recommence negotiations after a walk-out unless you specify when you will be back? Why not lower the temperature or significance of the walk-out by calling for an ADJOURN-MENT, even an abrupt one to "cool off", to "think about things", to seek advice, and so on. It is much easier to resume negotiations after an adjournment than after a walk-out.

"WE SHOULD HAVE BEEN TOLD"
A disavowal of responsibility ploy.

You have exceeded an agreed budget and want an additional payment for the extra work you have undertaken. They deny responsibility because "they should have been told" before you incurred extra expenses. As you did not tell them, they refuse to pay, no matter that the additional work was necessary. You are stuck with the cost.

Try to negotiate an official variation order system under which all variations to the contract must be authorised by a named official if payment is to be made, and in return, if an official variation order is made, the client guarantees payment of the extra costs.

Counter: Always tell them when extra work is required and do nothing until they agree. If the roof collapses before they agree, tell them that "you should have been told" that you had a blank cheque to do whatever was necessary.

"WHAT DO YOU KNOW?"
A long-shot ploy to elicit information.

The other negotiators open by asking you how much you know about the issues. You tell them. They find out more about your knowledge of the details than perhaps you intended to let them know at this stage. Your selection and presentation of detail also signals your PRIORITIES.

Counter: "Not a lot. Perhaps you could go over the issues for me?"

WHAT IF?
QUESTIONS to elucidate potential negotiable issues. Useful when faced with DEADLOCK. It helps to

explore possible solutions to the deadlock.

Q: What if we were to consider delaying the payment deadlines, would that help you with your budgeting?

Also useful when faced with a proposition that may look alright but you have no criteria against which to judge it.

Q: What if you make $200,000 instead of $50,000 in the first year? What larger share would I get in those circumstances?

A checklist of "what if?" questions drawn up before you negotiate is a useful PREPARATION tool.

WIN-WIN
I win, you win, so we both win. The goal of an effective negotiator (see NON-ZERO SUM).

In negotiating we have four possible outcomes defined in terms of winning or losing.

1	We both win.	3	I lose, you win.
2	I win, you lose.	4	We both lose.

We both lose in a DEADLOCK. The time spent negotiating could have been used for something more profitable, and we may experience long-term disagreeable consequences (litigation).

Either of us winning with the other losing is likewise an unattractive outcome. If I win at your expense (I sell you a failing business as a going concern), I risk destroying my reputation, or our relationship. If for any reason you are unhappy with the deal, or how we arrived at it, my winning is a Pyrrhic victory. It could cost me dear later.

The win-win outcome is the most desirable. It gives both of us a stake in the implementation of the AGREEMENT. On the basis of our experience, both of us are willing to consider doing more business in future and to pass on our helpful judgments about each other to third parties.

YES, BUT

A closing ploy.

"Your offer is acceptable, but for one small point." You meet the point in some way, and then expect agreement. "Fine. But there is this other detail we must settle." If you settle this issue, another one will pop up, and for as many acceptances as you make, they produce another "yes, but".

Counter: Identify all the reservations, and address them in one package.

- Exorcise the "yes, but".
- Retaliate with the "no but":

"I cannot accept movement on this small detail, but if you accept a change in this other point, I am prepared to consider a change in what you are now asking."

YESABLE PROPOSITION

A sellers' ploy based on the momentum generated by buyers saying "yes" to a series of proposals. If they keep saying yes they will eventually say yes to the closing proposition (in theory).

Q: You do have a problem with copying costs?
A: Yes.
Q: You accept that the Corex Copier copies more times per cent than any other on the market?
A: Yes.
Q: You want to start making big savings on copier costs right away?
A: Yes.
Q: Will you okay this request for a Corex Copier for delivery in 72 hours?
A: Yes.

It is not always so easy, but it is likely to be tried on you from time to time.

Counter: YES, BUT.

"YOU WIN SOME AND YOU LOSE SOME"

Do not underestimate the need to "save face"; it motivates almost everybody. You have put a lot of effort into an issue, argued long and strong for an outcome, perhaps even thrown in the odd THREAT or two, but in the end you realise you cannot get anything like what you want.

What do you do? Press on with the conflict? It is often better from the negotiator's point of view to admit defeat gracefully. Laugh it off:

- Well, George, you win some and you lose some, and this is not my winning day.
- That's life. It was worth trying.

ZERO SUM

Jargon from GAME THEORY: what you gain, they lose.

Your INTERESTS are diametrically opposed; you are in a state of pure conflict.

Some (difficult) negotiations and haggles are zero sum games (see NON-ZERO SUM). In pure conflict negotiations you perceive your opponent to be trying to gain at your direct expense. There can be no co-operation or collusion between you to find a mutually advantageous solution because all solutions (except your winning) are mutually disadvantageous.

ZEUTHEN'S CONFLICT AVOIDANCE MODEL

Compares the gains likely to be made by accepting what is on OFFER with the NET gains likely to be made by conflict (STRIKE or LOCK-OUT).

- There is a range of practicable bargains (the settlement range), and any wage rate within this range is more advantageous to either party than a conflict.
- Outside the settlement range ("the fighting sphere"), compromise is less advantageous than resort to conflict.
- The limits to fighting are given by the expected result of fighting plus or minus the expected fighting costs.
- The workers will not accept a wage rate lower than they could receive by a fight, less the losses they take by going on strike.
- The employers will not pay a wage higher than they could be forced to by a fight, plus the losses they take by contesting a strike.

Zeuthen's model is a two-stage process. The bargainers compare the certain value obtainable from accepting the other party's current offer with the expected value they obtain by holding to their current demand together with the expected value of a breakdown in the negotiations and mutual resort to conflict. This calculation produces the maximum probability of conflict they are willing to accept in preference to accepting the other side's current offer.

The bargainer whose willingness to accept the risk of conflict is smallest (the one who is most anxious to avoid conflict) is the one who makes the next concession. If it is the workers' AGENT, the union demand for a wage increase is reduced; if it is the employer, the company's offer of a wage rate is increased.

The size of a bargainers' CONCESSION is determined by how much a particular concession increases their willingness to risk a strike if it is unacceptable to the other side. Naturally, each party endeavours to persuade the other that any move short of the gap between them induces a preference for a strike (raising their apparent "eagerness for a fight" in the perception of their opponent).

Mistaken assessments of the other's eagerness for a fight, or miscalculations of your own net benefits of conflict, lead to a negotiated wage rate above or below what was practicable if the parties had made different assessments. It boils down to an assessment of which of the parties feels strong enough to resort to, or ride out, conflict.

Part 3

APPENDIXES

1 Negotiation training resources

The Negotiation Sourcebook,
Ira G. Asherman and Sandra
Vance Asherman, Human
Resource Development Press,
Amherst, Mass., USA, 1990.

*Negotiation Training Through
Gaming*, Elizabeth M.
Christopher and Larry E.
Smith, Kogan Page, London,
UK, 1991.

Negotiation: readings,
exercises, cases, Roy J.
Lewicki and Joseph A. Litterer,
Richard D. Irwin, Homewood,
Illinois, USA, 1985.

Harvard Negotiation Project
Harvard Law School
500 Pound Hall
Cambridge
Mass. 02138, USA

The Negotiation Style Profile,
Rollin Glaser and Christine
Glaser.
Management Learning
   Resources Limited
PO Box 28
Carmarthen
Dyfed SA31 1DT, UK
Tel: 0267 87661
Fax: 0267 87315

*Kennedy's Simulations for
Negotiation Training*, Gavin
Kennedy, January 1993.
Gower Training
Gower House
Croft Road
Aldershot
Hants GU11 3HR, UK
Tel: 0252 331 551
Fax: 0252 344 405

Negotiating Assertively,
Carolyn Richardson, 1990.
Pavilion Publishing (Brighton)
42 Lansdowne Place
Hove
East Sussex BN3 1HH, UK
Tel: 0273 821650

Computer based packages

The Negotiation Edge, for IBM
and compatibles.
Human Edge Software
   Corporation
2445 Faber Place
Palo Alto
California 94393, USA

The Art of Negotiation, for IBM
and compatibles.
Experience in Software Inc.
2000 Hearst Avenue
Suite 202
Berkeley
California 94709, USA
Tel: 415 644 0694
Fax: 071 240 5771

Distance learning package

Negotiation, Heriot-Watt
University MBA Series, 1991.
Pitman Publishing
128 Long Acre
London WC2E 9AN, UK
Tel: 071 379 7383

2 Video packages

The Art of Negotiation, 1983.
30 minutes; includes Trainer's
Guide and exercises.
Longman Training
Longman House
Burnt Mill
Harlow
Essex CM20 2JE, UK
Tel: 0279 623927
Fax: 0279 623795

Bargaining for Results. Four
videos, audio tape and
distance learning programme.
Winkler International Ltd
6 St George's Place
Brighton
East Sussex BN1 4GA, UK
Tel: 0273 676540
Fax: 0273 570133

Do We Have a Deal?, 1991. 25
minutes; includes Trainer's
Guide, participant's Notebook
and simulation.

Everything is Negotiable, 1988.
60 minutes; includes Trainer's
Manual plus participant's
guides, OHP slides and short
simulations.
Gower Training
Gower House
Croft Road
Aldershot
Hants GU11 3HR, UK
Tel: 0252 331 551
Fax: 0252 344 405

Meeting to Negotiate, 1991. 25
minutes; includes Training
Notes which incorporate some
short negotiating exercises.
BBC Enterprises
Woodlands
80 Wood Lane
London W12 0TT, UK
Tel: 081 576 2361
Fax: 081 749 8766

Negotiating Profitable Sales,
1982. Parts 1 and 2, 22 and 23
minutes respectively.
Video Arts
Dumbarton House
68 Oxford Street
London W1N 9LA, UK
Tel: 071 637 7288
Fax: 071 580 8103

3 Specialised consultants and trainers

Audis International Ltd
Kingfisher House
North Poulner Road
Ringwood
Hants BH24 1SN, UK
Tel: 0425 479 048
Fax: 0425 477 024

Chartered Institute of
  Marketing
Moor Hall
Cookham
Maidenhead
Berks SL6 9QH, UK
Tel: 06285 24922
Fax: 06285 22104

Coverdale Plc
Dorland House
14 Regent Street
London SW1Y 4PH, UK
Fax: 071 491 7636

Huthwaite Research Co. Ltd
Hobbert House
Wentworth
Rotherham
South Yorkshire S62 7SA, UK
Tel: 0709 710 081
Fax: 0709 710 065
Specialises in psychological
  negotiation

Industrial Society
3 Carlton House Terrace
London SW1Y 5AF, UK
Tel: 071 839 4300
Fax: 071 839 3898
Specialises in industrial
  relations and collective
  bargaining

Institute of Personnel
  Management
35 Camp Road
London SW19 4UX, UK
Tel: 081 946 9100
Fax: 081 947 2570
Specialises in industrial
  relations and collective
  bargaining

Invicta Training
240 Green Lane
New Eltham
London SE9 3TL, UK
Tel: 081 851 4044
Fax: 081 857 2443
Specialises in general
  negotiation

Karass UK
Arrowsmith Court
Station Approach
Broadstone
Dorset BH18 8AT, UK
Tel: 0202 848000
Fax: 0202 848008

USA
Tel: (310) 453 1806 or (310)
  828 4739
Japan
Tel: 0031 11 2401
Australia
Tel: 0014 800 128 610

Specialises in tactical ploys

Leadership Development Ltd
495 Fulham Road
London SW6 1HH, UK
Tel: 071 381 6233
Fax: 071 381 6915
Specialises in sales
  negotiations

The Mast Organisation
Hermitage House
Bath Road
Taplow
Maidenhead
Berks SL6 0AR, UK
Tel: 0628 784062
Fax: 0682 773061

Negotiate Limited
34 Argyle Place
Edinburgh EH9 1JT, UK
Tel: 031 228 8899
Fax: 031 228 8866
Specialises in negotiation
  training

The PDB Partnership
Jericho Farm
Cassington
Oxfordshire OX8 1EB, UK
Tel: 0865 883 400
Fax: 0865 883 901
Specialises in strategic
    negotiation consultancy

Purchasing and Supply
    Courses
Broom House
21 Chestnut Grove
Great Stukeley
Huntingdon
Cambs PE17 5AT, UK
Tel: 0480 414 103
Fax: 0480 431 529
Specialises in purchasing
    negotiations

Rose & Barton
Middle Gully Road
Macedon 3449
Victoria
Australia
Tel: (61) 54 26 1808
Fax: (66) 54 26 3048
General negotiations

Sayskills Limited
82a Wheturangi Road
Greenlane
Auckland
New Zealand
Tel: (64) 9 366 7930
Fax: (64) 9 266 0038
General negotiations

Winkler International Ltd
6 St George's Place
Brighton
East Sussex BN1 4GA, UK
Tel: 0273 676540
Fax: 0273 570133
Specialises in price
    negotiation

4 Recommended reading

Gerald Atkinson, *Negotiating the Best Deals*, Institute of Directors, London, 1990.

Max H. Bazerman and Margaret A. Neale, *Negotiating Rationally*, Macmillan, New York, 1992.

John A. Carlisle and Robert C. Parker, *Beyond Negotiation*, John Wiley, Chichester, 1989.

Herb Cohen, *How To Negotiate Anything*, Bantam Books, New York, 1973.

Roger Fisher and William Ury, *Getting to Yes*, Houghton Mifflin Co., Boston, 1981.

Marvin Gottlieb and William J. Healy, *Making Deals*, New York Institute of Finance, New York, 1990.

Harvard Law School, *Negotiation Journal* (quarterly), Plenum Publishing Corporation, 233 Spring Street, New York, NY, 10013, USA.

Donald W. Hendon and Rebecca Angeles Hendon, *How To Negotiate Worldwide*, Gower, Aldershot, 1989.

John Ilich and Barabara Schindler Jones, *Successful Negotiating Skills for Women*, Addison Wesley Publishing Company, Reading, Mass.,1981.

Chester Karass, *Give and Take*, Thomas Y. Crowell, New York, 1974.

Gavin Kennedy, *Everything is Negotiable* (2nd edition), Random House, London, 1990.

Gavin Kennedy, *The Perfect Negotiation*, Random House, London, 1992.

David A. Lax and James K. Sebenius, *The Manager as Negotiator*, The Free Press, New York, 1986.

John Lidstone, *Manual of Sales Negotiation*, Gower, Aldershot, 1991.

J.B. McCall and M.B. Warrington, *Marketing by Agreement* (2nd edition), John Wiley, Chichester, 1989.

P.D.V. Marsh, *Contract Negotiation Handbook* (2nd edition), Gower, Aldershot, 1984.

William F. Morrison, *The Pre-negotiation Planning Book*, John Wiley, New York, 1985.

J. Keith Murnighan, *Bargaining Games*, William Morrow Inc., New York, 1992.

Juliet Nierenberg and Irene S. Ross, *Women and the Art of Negotiating*, Simon & Schuster Inc., New York, 1985.

Gerald I. Nierenberg, *The Art of Negotiating*, Hawthorn Books, New York, 1973.

Howard Raiffa, *The Art and Science of Negotiation*, Harvard University Press, Mass., USA, 1982.

Colin Robinson, *Winning at Business Negotiations*, Kogan Page, London, 1990.

David L. Sheridan, *Negotiating Commercial Contracts*, McGraw-Hill, London, 1991.

Jeremy Thorn, *How To Negotiate Better Deals*, Mercury Books, London, 1989.

John Winkler, *Bargaining for Results*, Heinemann, London, 1982.